AFRICA'S HELL ON EARTH

The Ordeal of an African Journalist

AFRICA'S HELL ON EARTH:

The Ordeal of an African Journalist

Omar Bah

CENMEDRA

Published by CENMEDRA – the Centre for Media and Development Research in Africa

First published in the United States by TATE PUBLISHING AND EN-TERPRISES, LLC in 2014

This edition is published by CENMEDRA in The Gambia in 2018

www.cenmedra.org

ISBN: 9781693627149

Printed in Oxford, England

Front cover design by Sadibou Kamaso
Layout design: Folashade Lasisi JW
Cover photos: copyright@ CENMEDRA

www.cenmedra.org
info@cenmedra.org

Dedication

About the Author

Winner of the 2017 Red Bandana Award; and the 2016 John F. Kiffney Public Service Award from the Providence Newspaper Guild; Omar Bah is the Founder & Executive Director of the Refugee Dream Center based in Providence, in the state of Rhode Island, USA. He is a torture survivor, former journalist and refugee from The Gambia in West Africa. Bah is also a recipient of 'Rhode Islander of the Year 2015' award from Rhode Island Monthly Magazine. He represents the state of Rhode Island at the Refugee Congress at the United Nations High Commissioner for Refugees (UNHCR) in Washington, DC.

He holds a bachelor's degree in Communications Studies with a minor in political science from the University of Rhode Island; master's degree in Public Administration from Roger Williams University, and a master's in Counseling Psychology in Global Mental Health from William James College where he is currently pursuing a doctoral degree in Leadership Psychology in the Neuroscience of Psychology track. Bah has completed trauma treatment certification at the Harvard Program in Refugee Trauma (HPRT) and does trauma-based therapy. He currently teaches Psychology at HPRT and has taught Psychology at William James College. Omar was a 2017-Diversity Fellow at the Sherlock Center on Disabilities; and a Psychology Fellow at the Vermont Leadership Education in Neurodevelopmental Disabilities (LEND) for the 2018-19 academic year. He is a member of the Global Advisory Board of the Center for Human Rights & Humanitarian Studies at the Watson Institute for International & Public Affairs of Brown University.

Acknowledgements

This has not been an easy journey. Both the story told and the writing process have been difficult but very fulfilling to me. I am excited to have been able to reach this level. It would not have come to fruition if it were not for the support of my dear wife, Teddi Jallow. Since my escape from The Gambia in 2006, I have met exceedingly awesome people along the way. My particular gratitude goes to Amie Joof, the woman who hosted me in Senegal while I was in urgent need, and helped facilitate my move to Ghana. She took care of me as if I were her own son. I am hugely indebted to her. I am also grateful to many more people who have helped me to find a new life. My gratitude to Alhagie Mbye, Sheriff Bojang Junior, Ebrima Sillah, Musa Saidykhan, Agnes Thomasi, Pa Louis Thomasi, Demba A Jawo, Katia Wagner and many more. My Special thanks to Professor Kwame Karikari of the Accra-based Media Foundation for West Africa for all the support in relocating me to Ghana and for facilitating my eventual resettlement in America as a refugee, and my many generous Ghanaian friends. I also thank Sulayman Makalo for all the friendship and company in Ghana and beyond. Finally, I am thankful to America for giving me a home and hope when there was none. To my American friends, who gave me company and friendship when there was none, my hat off to you. I am particularly grateful to the entire staff of the International Institute of Rhode Island for helping me settle in America, and Rhode Island Housing, my first place of employment in America where I found so much comfort and love. My special thanks to some special friends – MaryAnn Lowe, Joann Noonan, Lynne Crowell, Ed Quinlan, Dr Dorothy Abram, Dr Robert Vanderslice, Dr Richard Mollica, and their respective families.

About CENMEDRA

CENMEDRA – the Centre for Media and Development Research in Africa – is a knowledge centre. Registered as an educational charity in The Gambia on 3 March 2014 it aims to promote, facilitate and disseminate research in media, communication and development in Africa. Its activities are focused on five main areas namely media research, researching development, new media and society, education, and publication. In line with its underlying aim of research application, it shares its research results with policymakers, media and development practitioners, media houses, regulators, scholars, politicians, librarians, activists, donors, development agencies, and the wider research community. It has a two-tiered governance structure: a board of trustees drawn from the media, civil society and academia, which provides strategy and policy direction, and an administrative secretariat that is responsible for operations and policy implementation.

MISSION
CENMEDRA exists to foster innovative research that puts Africa on the path of peace, progress and prosperity.

VISION
CENMEDRA envisions an enlightened African society, free from the burden of ignorance, where everyone is able to realise their fullest potential in peace and prosperity.

VALUES
Integrity
Openness
Creativity
Diligence

Problems are solved by *thinking*, not by a special method.

(Adapted from Thomas, G., 2011, p.6)

"There is only one good – knowledge, and one evil – ignorance."
Socrates (circa 470-399BC)
http://www.cenmedra.org
Email: info@cenmedra.org

Prologue

I had barely worked one year in journalism when I had my first taste of its inherent hazards. I was merely 21 years old at the time. One morning, while I was at work at *The Independent*, the telephone in the newsroom rang. The caller asked for me. When I took the phone, the caller said, "Hello, Mr Bah! Good! In fact, you are the one we are looking for!"

The caller was with someone else and I could hear him or her whispering in the background.

When I asked who he was, he told me that he was a soldier wanting to give me a tip about a top government secret, and thus could not disclose his name. According to the caller, a secret court martial of a former commander of the presidential guards who was accused of treason was going on, and they feared if the public did not know about it, the soldier in question could be killed. He maintained that the secret trial was meant as a smokescreen against accusations of summary executions, as the government could easily present records of the court-martial to neutralize any international investigation.

The two voices whispered between themselves for a short while, before one of them spoke again.

"Listen, Mr Bah. The two of us are concerned soldiers. We just wanted to inform you that Lt Landing Sanneh will be at the Yundum Barracks for the court martial. The first sitting is scheduled for tomorrow at 10:00 am. You cover the courts, so you may want to follow up on this. Please make sure you let the public know about it."

"Thank you very much for that information. We will definitely put it to the public knowledge," I said.

Lt Landing Sanneh, the soldier who was being secretly court martialled, had been shot several times during his arrest while other soldiers who were alleged to have taken part in the same attempted coup were killed in cold blood. Some were shot in broad daylight in public places. Yet while others were shot and killed as they hid themselves in the open market in Banjul.

"Thank you, sir,Mr Bah. But sorry we cannot identify ourselves. It's too dangerous," one of them said.

"I understand. Thank you once again for your courage."

As soon as I put down the phone, I noted in my mini notebook the name of the military barracks and the time the court martial was to begin. I felt challenged because somebody's life was hanging in the balance – and the fact that the public had recognized me as a court reporter and had hopes in me spurred me on. I rushed into the office of the editor in such haste that he immediately knew I was up to something big. Because my managing editor, Alagi Yorro

Jallow, was a news maniac, reporters mocked him behind his back that "he thinks news is food". Then again, he recognized that this particular assignment was dangerous and asked repeatedly whether I felt up to it. When he saw my unbridled zeal, he gave his blessing and with that I hit the ground running.

The following morning, July 12, 2001, I set out to Yundum Barracks with a mini tape recorder and a small notebook in my pocket. I did not take a bag. I wanted to be as discreet as possible. As soon as I entered the gates, a group of soldiers confronted me – all their guns pointing at me. One of them asked me to explain why I was inside the barracks. When I opened my mouth to explain, he stopped me and asked me to follow him. The other soldiers followed us while still pointing their guns at me. Another soldier in red beret appeared from a building. He looked like he was the head of the group as he commanded the group to a halt.

The red-beret soldier asked me why I was there, and I told him I was there to cover the court martial proceedings as a reporter. As soon as I mentioned the word 'reporter', he asked me to produce an identification to prove I was who I claimed to be. I gave him my press card, which he looked at and then showed to another soldier standing next to him. Both of them mumbled something before he turned to me and said:

"You are Omar Bah? You think you are the bravest among all the journalists to come here?" He was now sitting but sprang up again. The name on his tag read 'Fullo Jallow'. He threw my press card on the ground. When I picked it up, I realized that the group of soldiers – over a dozen of them – had closed in on me. Fullo Jallow, the red-beret soldier, made a beckoning sign with his head to the rest of the soldiers. As I tried to turn in an attempt to leave the barracks, a huge bang hit my head. It was a gun butt. It felt like the earth was swirling around. The rest of the group pounced on me. They kept hitting me with gun butts and kicking me with their boots while hauling insults at me. Sometimes, they would lift me and toss me in the air and, when I was heading to the ground, they would hit me with gun butts and kick me until I landed. I was bleeding profusely. My shirt was soaked in blood. I cried until I lost my voice. They continued hitting me until I could no longer move my body. Then they carried me and dumped me inside a little cell at the back of a building.

I did not know whether it was a store or a closet, but it was so tiny that I had to curl myself into a fetus position in order to fit in. When it was locked, it was so dark that I could not even see my fingers. The torrid summer weather was at its worst. I was so wet that I could not tell whether the continuous precipitation from my body was blood or sweat. The smell inside the cell was terrible. Little rats, geckos and lizards were running on me and making some noises. Mosquitoes had a field day on me. I thought I was going to die. From time to time, one or two soldiers would open the door, perhaps to see if I was still alive, start kicking and hitting me with gun butts until I was completely motionless again before they would lock the door and leave.

I remained in that condition until later that evening when a certain soldier in the barracks came and opened the door. I thought it was one of the routine torturers. When he asked me to follow him, I tried to get up, but fell back on the floor. Even when he supported me with his hand, I still could not walk properly. He therefore ordered a group of soldiers to lift and put me on a bench in a corner of a room in the building. It took me a while before I could take in my surroundings.

When I was released, I went to the Serrekunda Health Centre but was refused treatment until and unless I submitted a police report. I decided against going to the police for obvious reasons and instead went to see my grandmother who bought some ointment and pain killers from a drug store to treat me. Even when other hospitals and health centers turned us down the following day, my grandmother resorted to alternative medicine like local herbs to treat me.

There had been a serious reaction to my beating by both the local press and the international community. My editors told me that someone had seen the soldiers surround me when I first entered the barracks that morning of the attack and sensed that I was in danger. As a result, that person, a journalist himself, contacted my editors who in turn kept pressure on the military command until I was released. In the next edition of the *Independent*, I wrote about my encounter with the military. A local newspaper interviewed me and wrote about the issue. International media organizations heated up the campaign against the violation. I received a call from the New York-based Committee to Protect Journalists (CPJ) that interviewed me about the incident. The CPJ later issued a press release condemning the attack. The pressure on the military was mounting. A lawyer who was a friend of mine, threatened to help me sue the military pro bono. One day, the army headquarters called my editors and asked for a meeting between us. One of my editors, Demba Ali Jawo, went with me to the army headquarters. We did not know what exactly to expect but we were told that we would be meeting with the head of the national army and his deputy. We alerted everyone in the office so that they knew where we were.

At the meeting, the military chiefs apologized. In the newspaper publications about my attack and detention, the name of the soldier whose tag read 'Fullo Jallow' was highly publicized. Therefore, during the meeting with the military chiefs, he was brought in and asked to apologize to me, which he did. At the end of the meeting, my editor demanded that the military issue a public apology and to give me unhindered access to the trial that I had attempted to cover with assurance of my safety. The chiefs initially hesitated about the public apology, but we said that we were not going to back off. After a little effort, when they realized that we were not ready to budge, they agreed. Before we left the building, they had already prepared me with a press pass that they said I should always carry when I was at the barracks. The card was pink-colored and had the inscriptions:

> The Gambia Armed Forces
> Press Pass
> Omar Bah

The military high command subsequently issued the public apology, which was published across the media. In addition, I was given access to the barracks to cover the proceedings of the court-martial. I never saw Fullo Jallow again. Some media houses had also applied for a press pass and their reporters were going with me to the trial. The soldier who was facing the treason trial was jailed for sixteen years rather than being executed.

Because my family feared reprisals of some sort, they pressured me to quit journalism and take up something else.

1

A call came to my cell phone. It was Ebrima Baldeh, a friend who worked at the national television. He did not greet and sounded nervous: "Omar! There is trouble!"

"What?" I said.

"Your friend who is living abroad..., that one who is writing those critical things against the head of this place," he said, sounding even more nervous. Apparently, he was doing the best he could to avoid mentioning the name of Pa Nderry M'bai, the editor of the USA-based online *Freedom* newspaper, and that of the Gambian leader, Yahya Jammeh whom he obliquely referred to as 'head of this place'– 'this place' meaning The Gambia.

"I understand, boy, please go ahead, I'm curious," I said.

"Well, something serious is going on. He has defected to the side of the 'head of this place' and has announced publicly that he will never write against him and will be campaigning for him in the upcoming elections."

"What?" I said. I did not realize that I had raised my voice so high that I had caught everyone's attention. I was standing in the middle of the computer room of the *Daily Observer* newspaper where I worked.

The *Daily Observer* is the largest and first daily newspaper in the country. However, over the years, it has steadily fallen on to government censorship and has ended up as a propaganda tool for the dictatorial regime. It is located on a one-storey building on a major intersection in Bakau, a few miles away from the capital city, Banjul. There is hardly a journalist of repute in The Gambian who has not passed through the *Daily Observer* at some point in their career. These include Demba Ali Jawo, Baba Galleh Jallow, Sheriff Bojang, Sheriff

Bojang Junior, Ndey Tapha Sosseh, Bai Emil Touray, Pa Nderry M'bai, and Cherno Baba Jallow. The upbeat and progressive atmosphere that once prevailed at the *Daily Observer* has however evaporated because career-minded journalists now distance themselves from the degradation the paper has become in terms of professionalism and commitment to serving the cause of the Gambian people.

"Boy, I'm not ready with what I'm saying yet. Do you know what he did?" He paused. Then he said: "He provided a list of people who he said used to give him privileged information about the 'head of this place'. That is why I am calling you because I know you are among his closest friends and, given your stubbornness, you might have been one of his reporters from here. Moreover, that means your name could be there. Everybody can see the list on the website right now. You had better see whether your name is there before you get into trouble."

I was dumbfounded. My legs felt like lead; I could not move from where I was standing. Suddenly, I crashed into a chair and pressed my head with both hands. My mind was in a whirl from what I had just heard. I told myself that Pa Nderry could not have possibly betrayed me—and all the Gambians who are fighting against this tyranny. How could he have been so cruel as to supply our names to the tyrant? If he really did, then that meant death for me because I had written about the tyrant in the *Freedom* newspaper on a wide range of issues, notably assassinations and corruption in high places. Then someone, a lady in the computer room broke into my reverie, and asked, "Are you Okay?" I cannot remember answering her. In a daze, I ambled out of the computer room into the main hall and strode on the corridor. Then I bounded down the staircase, veered left and rushed to a cybercafé, a few meters away from the premises of the Daily Observer. The list my friend who called earlier mentioned was not there. Instead, on the website was another story – a message from the editor of the newspaper himself, Pa Nderry M'bai. He informed the general readership that an earlier message posted on his website with a list of purported informants was the work of a hacker hired by the dictatorship in The Gambia. He said he had neither stopped publishing the *Freedom* newspaper nor had he defected to the government. He explained that the said list was a mere list of email subscribers. He warned the government not to harm any of such persons because none of them was a reporter for him and that if they did, they would be harming people whose only crime was reading a newspaper. Finally, he assured his readership that he had regained control of his website from the hacker and was resolved to continue to "rattle the cage" of the dictator, President Yahya Jammeh.

While still at the cybercafé, I received a call on my cell phone again. It was

Mam Sait Ceesay, who doubled as editor-in-chief of the *Daily Observer* and as press officer at the Office of the President. Because he was a close ally of the tyrant, I suspected that the call might be about the *Freedom* newspaper issue. "Omar!" his husky voice boomed down the phone. I listened keenly to his tone, trying to make out the motive for his call. I sensed that he suspected me of being involved with the *Freedom* newspaper.

"Yes?" I said. "Where are you?"

"I'm around." I avoided saying where exactly I was.

"Do you know the *Freedom* newspaper; have you heard that name?" he asked. I hesitated for a while, not knowing what his real motive was or what to say.

"Yes".

"Are you a reporter for them?" I did not answer.

"Well," he said. "The President gave me a list of people who have been re-porting for Pa Nderry of the *Freedom* newspaper. I have just one thing to say: the president will seriously deal with anyone who is part of this. The president gave it to me to publish it because it was given to him as a birthday gift. Well, you said you are not their reporter, but more information is coming other than this list. We'll know if you are involved, and we will deal with anyone one that we catch."

I put my phone down, pretending that the phone had some network connec-tion problem. I was scared. I was trembling so hard on the chair. It seemed I had to be extremely careful. My name could either be on the list or not on it – and if my name was not on the so-called list, why was my boss already treat-ing me like a suspect? My head throbbed with wild imaginings.

The night before, I had had a nightmare: *I am on my way to my village, Sam -Mbollet, to visit my mother and relatives as I often do. It is very late in the night. There is no sign of any human being. When I alight from the commercial transport in the village of Njongon, everyone is asleep. Aside from the occa-sional barks of dogs, and hootings of owls, there is no other noise. As I begin walking toward my village, I look back and see the huge Kulenteng[1] tree in the centre of the primary school I attended several years earlier when I was much younger. It sends me back to some of my childhood friends and teachers, and the wonderful moments I have had there as a child. I continue walking toward my village, Sam-Mbollet, which is situated a few miles away–into the bush. I have never been afraid of that distance. However, when I look at the time on my cell phone, it is about 1am. It is so dark that I cannot even see my fingers when I lift up my arm. Nevertheless, I keep walking determined to go on, no matter what. I have not seen my mother for some time now so I am determined to see her before I go to sleep this particular night. Therefore, I keep walking.*

In the distance, I hear intermittent howls of hyenas. That is normal. A small forest marks the boundary between Njongon and Sam-Mbollet. That is the only place that scares me. As soon as I pass that place, I am relieved. However, I run into unexpected danger. The forest is now behind me, and I am left with the remaining half of the journey. Something jumps in front of me. It is so dark that I cannot figure out what it exactly is. All I know is that it is a scary and dangerous-looking animal. It is only when it starts jumping up and down, blocking my way and howling that I realize my life is in danger because a hyena is about to attack me. I cannot escape. There is only one little Dooki[2] tree nearby where I can climb, and the hyena happens to block my access to it. Bar- ing its teeth at me, the hyena lifts its forelegs, runs around me, and strews me all over with dust.

When I told my mother about the dream in the morning, she reassured me to be strong even though it portended a negative development. I sat in front of the computer in the cybercafé, holding my head with both hands, lost in thought. I knew I was in a quagmire and had to act fast before the tyrant's mad dogs pounced on me. I decided to call my mother. Having made up my mind on what to do, I ran across the road to the telecenter opposite the *Daily Observer* office. I dialed my mother's number. "Daa[3]!" I said. I must have screamed. "What is it, Omar, you are scaring me?" she said.

"You are right. It's indeed scary. I just want to tell you that something serious is going on; something that can put me in big trouble at any time. But I just need one thing from you: just pray for me, Daa. Pray for me. It has to do with my journalism work, but I hope it doesn't come to the worst."

"Okay, Omar Bittaye." She calls me by the full name of my namesake when she wants to praise or console me. "You will be fine, okay. What is it about?"

I explained to her, and she told me not to talk to people around since trusting too many people could be dangerous too. She prayed for me again. I dropped the phone, promising to call later to update her on what was going on with me. As I walked out of the tele-center, I raised up my arms in the air, said "amen" to my mother's prayers and rubbed my hands on my face.

I had to do something. Apart from my name, there was another name that came to my mind that I thought could be on the list – Ousman Darboe, one of the reporters at the *Daily Observer* where I was news editor.

I thought he was independent-minded and critical enough to have been secretly reporting for the *Freedom* newspaper. None of the reporters of that US-based website knew one another. Only the editor in America knew who his reporters were. I called Ousman on his cell phone. When he received my call, he knew right away that something was wrong. He asked why I had called him. I told him that the government was out to harm all the people associated with the *Freedom* newspaper and warned him that if he thought he had once reported for *Freedom* newspaper, he should be as cautious as possible. He told me that he had never reported for that newspaper. I told him that I was not sure if my own name would be on the so-called list but I urged him to return to the office quickly so that both of us could take a snoop on the list that Mr Ceesay had promised to bring along that evening. That way we felt we would be able to know what to do if our names were on the list. He agreed and rushed back to the office immediately. Before the editor-in-chief gave the list to the staff in the computer room to type, Ousman and I sneaked it to the balcony under the overhanging branches of a mango tree and went through it. Our names were not on the list. With this, I really believed that Pa Nderry had not betrayed others and me and that this was the work of a government hacker. I knew if it were a list of reporters of the said newspaper, my name would probably stand more prominent than anyone else's. Ousman told me he had information that some people had already been arrested just because they were subscribers of the paper. When the list appeared in the *Daily Observer* on Friday, May 26, 2006, the police issued a follow-up press release ordering anyone whose name had been published to report to the nearest police station or risk prosecution. That day and the day after, the police arrested and detained scores of people.

I received a call from my father asking whether I was safe. I had not spoken to him about what was going on as I did with my mother, yet he knew that since the whole pandemonium had to do with the media, I was a potential victim. I told him that I was fine and that I would inform him if I sensed any danger. I called my wife, Teddi, who was now living in another town where she attended school. I told her nothing about what was going on, because I did not want to scare her. Later that evening, as I had planned, I attended the meeting with the *W aato* magazine [I did part time reporting for that cultural magazine] staff at the Badala Park hotel. At the end of the meeting, Sainabou Fofana [my colleague at the magazine who did the adverts layout for us] and her husband gave me a ride and dropped me on Kairaba Avenue by the junction of the Africell building. I was heading to my village. A friend of mine was having a bride welcoming ceremony that I could not afford to miss.

2

The late arrival of the ferry delayed my journey. When I reached Njongon from where I would trek a few miles into the bush to reach my village, Sam-Mbollet, it was already pitch dark. I remembered the nightmare I had had just a night earlier and here I was in real life doing just like it appeared in the dream. I stopped briefly, prayed, rubbed my hands over my face and proceeded, hoping that no hyena would get in my way. When I got to the village, it was very noisy. Music was blasting out all over the place, and the venue of the ceremony, as well as the streets leading to it, were full of people going up and down. I headed straight to my family compound. It was silent there. As usual, the dog barked at me. The children in the compound used to tease me that I was now a stranger, as according to them, the dog barked at only strangers. I whistled and called out his name, Arrgony, and waved. Nevertheless, he would still not believe that I was part of the compound. As he got more and more aggressive and potentially dangerous, a kerosene lamp was lit in my mother's house. I could barely see her as she opened the door in the dark. However, I could easily recognize her gait. She is fairly dark in complexion and is a soft-spoken woman who is average in height. She walks slowly and is also averagely slim.

She called out in a low voice, "Omar." She immediately opened the door, and asked Arrgony to stop making a noise. It was only then he stopped barking and moved away.

"How did you know it was me, Daa?"

I should not have asked for several reasons. My mother knew I was notorious for coming late at night; she, like everyone else, expected me to grace the

6

ceremony; and she knew if it had been a stranger, he or she would have left the compound as the dog howled unabated.

"Who else would it be? Come in and eat." I followed her into the house. There were so many people sleeping on the sitting room bed, and on mats on the floor that I had to pick my way gingerly over and around the sprawling figures on the floor. They were among the guests at the bride-welcoming ceremony, some of whom are my aunts. Daa gave me two bowls of food—one was rice and the other couscous. I tried the rice but was not interested. I then tried the couscous; I was interested but could not eat much. I was full and just wanted to chat with Daa a bit and then proceed to the ceremony.

"So where is your bag?" "I came like this."

"Omar, when will you stop being strong-headed and not come here late at night?"

"Daa, I cannot just help it, but I will work hard on it. How is the ceremony going?"

"It's very exciting. People have been asking of you throughout the day. They have even lost hope that you will turn up. They will be surprised and happy when they see you."

"I'm heading there now. We will talk in the morning, Daa." "Wait, I will go with you. The programme is full of people, perhaps
I can watch the dancing, too."

"You'll make them start teasing me again." I laughed as we walked. Many of the people in the village had noticed the obsessive closeness between my mother and me. A lot of them, including some of my friends, usually tease that my mother thought I was still a little baby. Each time I was with my friends and they predicted that my Daa would either come to call me or send somebody else to do so, it always happened. Moreover, they would laugh about it because their prediction had come true. The women at the compound of the Turrka tribe made a whole lot of fun out of it. Whenever my friends and I gathered there, the women would thank me for coming, as they had no doubt that my Daa or her representative would soon be in town. In addition, it always happened. Many people knew about this filial fondness between my mother and me, and they joked incessantly about it. Nevertheless, I never joined the jokes they made about my mother because I was not sure who between the two of us really encouraged this 'baby-sitting' thing. Sometimes when I went on weekends, especially during huge village festivals, I would stay indoors throughout, keeping my Daa company. Many people in the village would only see me or know that I was in fact there, when I was on my way back to the city and passed them with Daa accompanying me. Seen in this way, I am much as responsible as Daa in nurturing this relationship.

When we reached the venue of the ceremony, some of Daa's age bracket had already sat in groups around the compound entrance, watching the dancers. I greeted them, and they all teased about my Daa's 'baby-sitting' attitude. Then I left her there and proceeded to join my friends. They were ecstatic when they saw me. One of them, Modou, took me to his house and offered me milk with couscous. He said he had kept it especially for me. I went with him to the bride's house. There were many people milling around, some were strangers, others were locals. They were playing Fula violin music in their stereo. It seemed everyone was waiting for me. Some of them jumped on me and hugged me. The bride knew me well. On most occasions that the groom, Demba, used to go to the bride's village after their marriage in the past year, I used to accompany him there. Therefore, many of the guests knew me. The bride introduced me to the ones I did not know.

Demba, the groom, was very thankful that I had made it. He recounted to me all that had happened in the ceremony so far. I apologized that I had to come late and assured him that I would be by his side for the rest of the night. He told me not to mind and said that the place felt lonely in my absence. All the compounds of the Fulas and those of the neighboring Sererrs were occupied by the guests. However, my friend, Modou who lived in the same compound as Demba, had prepared his sitting room for me to pass the night. I took along some of my friends who could fit to share the place with me. The following morning, he got some milk for me from his herd of cattle. His wife gave me water in a bucket of water at the straw bathroom at the back of the house to take a bath. I then joined him and others to drink green tea before my mother, as usual, sauntered in to take me home, making everyone laugh about it.

That day, a Saturday, was the last of the three-day ceremony. Unknown to me, some elders in the village had conferred on me the honor to be the 'Father of Tongues' during the usual last late evening gathering. With such responsibility, I would be the closest person to the groom and should always be by his side. All communications between him and the rest of the people were to pass through me. I was exhilarated because it was the first time I had taken up such a traditional responsibility.

Lanky and fair complexioned, the groom, Demba, is just about three years older than I am and is an electrician by profession. He and I sat down in front of the gathering at the compound courtyard. The bride accompanied by some elderly women was to share gifts among the guests. She began with her husband and me by kneeling down in front of us and handing us each pieces of beautiful blankets. After so many cycles of traditional rites and gift giving, the next phase of it began. The elders were to advice bride and groom. In addition, when they addressed the groom, they would address both him and me directly, implying that I should as clearly get the message too so that if he made mistakes in his marital life, I could help him amend his ways. My father spoke first among the elders. After all the elders said what they had to talk to us about, the groom and I were asked to leave. Some elderly women beckoned me to lead the groom into his house. We were the only two to leave the gathering. The bride was also to be counseled, and many other ceremonial activities were yet to be done. I entered the house first. Demba detoured and walked straight to Modou's house. Some of the girls who came from the bride's village were waiting in the bedroom. As I greeted them and stood nearby, they asked me where Demba was. I pointed in the direction he had gone but promised them that he would be back soon. Before I could turn my head and look for a place to sit and listen to their violin music, the girls had surrounded me and rubbed me with some stinky stuff. Just then, I realized why Demba had run away. I noticed he was smiling when he was leaving, but I did not suspect anything. He knew I did not know about that trick and wanted me to experience it so that he could laugh at my expense. The essence of this prank is to test the temperament of the groom and the 'Father of Tongues'. Now that Demba was gone, I knew the girls would relish pasting my body and clothes with all the mess. I had changed into a white shirt for the ceremony. The girls so rubbed me with that muddy stuff that the white shirt suddenly looked like it was a tie-dyed material. As they were doing that, two older women rushed into the house saying, "It's enough! Leave him alone".

I was breathless with relief. The women gave me water to clean my face and asked me to turn over my shirt so that when I went outside, people would not notice the mess. Then they led me outside. I avoided the attention of the crowd and headed straight to Modou's house. As soon as Demba saw me, he burst into uncontrollable laughter. I narrated how the girls ambushed and jeered me. While we were laughing, my mother who was sitting among the crowd and had noticed something was going on with me, walked in and asked that I accompanied her to our compound. By then Modou and some of the boys were around, and I left the groom with them promising to return later to resume my responsibility as the 'Father of Tongues'. My mother did not even ask what happened, because she knew.

"Why didn't you head straight home and change your clothes?" she said. "Well, I wanted to avoid catching the attention of the people." I said, as we arrived at our compound, where I changed and remained for a long time.

It was not until the groom himself and some other friends came for me that I returned to the venue of the ceremony.

On Sunday morning, Daa and her sister, Jabou, called me inside Daa's bedroom to talk about my safety and the media situation in the country. I explained to them in detail what was going on and how dangerous it was. They both warned me to be extra careful. Daa recounted how she had been having sleep- less nights since the *Freedom* newspaper saga began. I promised them both that I would take heed to their advice. Before that, my father had also called me to his house for a similar conversation.

Overwhelmed by the conversations I had had with my family, I was in no mood to return to Banjul and resume work. To while away the time, I carried my nine-month old niece in my arms and went to the grocer's in a nearby compound, where I bought two lollipops, gave her one, and took the other for myself. I sat on a low stool on my mother's veranda and placed her on my lap. I would occasionally put my lollipop in her mouth. Then I would demand that she do the same for me too, which she did with glee. It was very comforting to be with her. I had missed her badly and since I came two days earlier, I had not really had time for her. I wished I were going to be with her the whole day, but I could not. I had to go back to the city, to work. Some of my mother's relatives, including Jabou, were returning home the same day, too. We were all going home on the same route.

However, I delayed them. I just sat on the veranda, procrastinating. I kept rocking my niece and listening to a tape of Fula violin. My father brought out two new cassettes of the singer, Assan, which I had not heard before. They were a combination of tracks some of which had been done in our compound during the naming ceremony of my niece, some months earlier. I kept listening to the cassettes for a long time. Any time I wanted to get up and go, I would feel lazy and just wish I would not be returning to the city. A commercial transport came to town. It was taking passengers by the gate of the venue of the just-ended ceremony. My aunt, Jabou, and the other visitors who stayed in our compound left to join it. I told them I preferred to walk later to the nearby village of Njongon to pick transport at my own time. It was around midday now. Finally, even Daa, who normally would not want me to leave her alone, encouraged me to go back to Banjul. She asked me to take along the two new cassettes my father had given me and that she would tell him about my taking them later. I put them in my pocket. I bade farewell to my niece and everybody. Daa and Ousainou, my eight-year-old sibling, and the last of my mother's eight children, accompanied me to the edge of our compound.

The commercial transport was still around. I walked toward it. Midway, I heard someone calling my name. It was Daa. She did not stop at the edge of the compound but had followed me instead. We both walked together to the vehicle. My friends, Modou and Demba, met me around the vehicle and bade farewell. Some women in the compound and in the car teased Daa of her 'baby-sitting' habit yet again, and we all laughed about it. I was happy though, that I was now finally going to be on the same journey with my aunt. As my mother bade farewell and started walking away, I called her, got down the vehicle, and met her outside. I gave her some money to send to one of her distant half elder sisters who had asked me to help her buy curtains.

"Oh Omar, she will be very happy. I thought you even forgot about it, or maybe you did not have it. Thank you for being so thoughtful. She will pray for you. Have a safe journey! Make sure you are careful, okay. I will keep my prayers for you."

"Bye, Daa."

The driver had lost patience and had begun revving his engine. As soon as I hopped into the vehicle, he sped away, as if deliberately halting the never-ending farewell between Daa and me. She kept looking back at the vehicle as she walked away and both of us waving at each other until the vehicle turned down a bend and I lost sight of her.

I felt despondent, as the vehicle sped away. Then I looked back at Sam-Mbollet to reminisce its scenic splendors. Sam-Mbollet is a small settlement in the northwest of the country. Less than ten miles to the Atlantic Ocean, the village stands in the middle of everywhere, yet it seems to be in the middle of nowhere. This uniqueness makes the village somehow different from many other neighboring villages. Unlike many linear villages with compounds lining the roads, Sam-Mbollet is right in the heart of the bushes. Off close to two miles from the nearest road that leads to the border with Senegal, the village is somehow isolated. Most settlers prefer living in the linear villages on the roadsides for obvious mobility reasons. Thus, Sam-Mbollet is one of the smallest in the region as most settlers usually go there as a last resort. Advantageously, the village has a lot of farmland and pastures to offer. Thus, it has steadily expanded over the years and now has about twenty compounds. Aside from the few new cement structures, the village is a hotchpotch of mud huts and rusted corrugated iron roofs.

At the village center is a huge courtyard filled with white sand similar to those found on beaches. That is where children play soccer in the afternoon and other games such as wrestling and hide and seek or dance to music or drumbeats at night. I had enjoyed all these pastimes when I was growing up there. From the same village center, dirt roads lead off in every direction. To the east of the village is the dirt road leading to Ndofan village, and to the south is the one leading to Berending, while the road to the west leads to Mbollet-Ba. To the northwest is Njongon, our nearest neighbor. Children from my village trek the three-kilometer distance every morning to attend school there. I also did the same for many years during my childhood. A host of other paths break out in every direction heading to farms, the nearby stream or the surrounding forests. A ring of forest belt surrounds Sam-Mbollet, which makes it ideal for the cultivation of peanuts, coos, corn, cassava et cetera. During the rainy season, children usually stay in the farms to watch out for the monkeys so that they do not destroy the crops. In addition, there are several groves of mango trees besides the other domestic and fruit trees strewn around the village. In the forests nearby, there are plenty of wild animals most of which are hunted for meat.

There are numerous herds of cattle. In the dry season, donkeys, goats, sheep, and chicken roam the streets and courtyards, while horses peer through the stables and neigh when disturbed. Burning straw on the farmlands sometimes pollute the environment. By contrast, the aromas that waft from the kitchens coupled with the wisps of smoke that curl across the sky give an ethereal quality to the village.

When we reached the town of Barra, the crossing point of the River Gambia, my aunt Jabou invited me to her home. She knew I was in no mood to return to Banjul that day. She asked whether I wanted to pass by her house and have lunch before proceeding on my journey. I went with her. When we reached her home, she gave me a coal pot and a little metal kettle to brew green tea. In addition, she gave me a stereo to play music to entertain myself. I pulled the two cassettes from my jeans pocket and played them while I prepared the green tea.

During the time I was in Barra, my colleagues at work called me constantly, asking whether I was safe. They were concerned because I did not show up at work, as I should have been there for work on the Monday edition of the *Daily Observer* newspaper. It was not until when it was really getting late and dark that I rushed to the terminal to catch one of the last ferries returning to the city.

3

On the morning of Monday, May 29, 2006, the day after I had returned from the village, I woke from my sleep and sat in the middle of the bed. The first thing I did was look at the time on my cell phone. It was almost 8 a.m. and I was certain that before I got to work that morning, it would be one or two hours later. However, that was my work routine because some editorial staff and I usually stayed late at work and thus should not be expected to go to work the same time as the rest of the normal staff. After checking the time, I continued to sit in the middle of the bed.

I had had a nightmare again: *I am on a journey, wandering in a thick and dark forest. The forest is laden with thick canopies and strange sounds. I walk for a long time without seeing any village or human. I am terrified to the brink. However, I keep walking. Finally, I see myself at the edge of the forest, and can see in the distance, the skyscrapers of a very beautiful and modern city. I am astonished at the sight, as I have never seen such kind of city in my life. I walk in the direction of the city. It is still a distance away, but I am sure with perseverance, I will get there. There is a vast green land belting the city. Just on the outskirts of it, I see a large group of hyenas. I have never seen these many hyenas in my life either. Moreover, three things surprise me about them: they are all white in color; they are grazing grass that hyenas normally do not do; and they have all turned their backs on me with none of them looking at me or even noticing my presence. I stop for a brief moment, thinking whether to turn back or proceed. Nevertheless, I realize that I am indeed safe. I proceed into the city. Just as I enter, I wake up.*

As I sat in the middle of the bed mulling over the dream, it did not make sense to me. I pulled out my cell phone and wanted to call my mother, but I felt lazy and let it go. I just did not want to think or talk about hyenas anymore. However, I was feeling very tired and depressed. Despite the hot and sunny weather, I was feeling cold. I thought I was getting sick. I wore a sweater, carried my bag and headed to work.

About an hour after I reported to work, I walked down to the cybercafé near the *Daily Observer* offices to go online and see what might have been happening while I was in the village. The US-based website at the center of the hacking debacle, *Freedom* newspaper, had been publishing about the detention and torture of its subscribers and all the developments that had been unfolding in relation to that. I checked my email and found that the website editor had written to me the day before. I was curious to know what he had said but I was extremely cautious. Before opening the email, I looked around to make sure that no one in the cybercafé could see what I was reading. The email read: What's up Mr. Bah? I hope you are safe and okay. Please keep us posted about developments. This government is a joke. They are hell bent on trying to blackmail the *Freedom* Newspaper, but they will woefully fail. They are angered by our revealing stories and they think that the best way to confuse our readers is to 'cook up' a story against my very self and the paper. But they are now exposed. Their attempts to ground the paper failed. The paper is back to business. Don't give up. Keep sending your pieces. We want to wire you some money, but we need to get some info from you before sending it. I will try to call you. Please get back to me....

It would be great if you can cover the so-called police arrests for us and tell us what the latest situation is. They are arresting the wrong people. These are mere subscribers and not sources as bandied by the Observer and the government. I sent a rejoinder to the Observer, The Point and *Foroyaa* to set the records [sic] straight. I doubt if the pro-government [paper] will run our reaction. Well, history will judge those behind this misinformation and lies against our paper. Have a great day.

I found the email very reassuring and encouraging. I had now officially heard from the editor himself and was more than certain that his email account had been hacked. More importantly, I was more resolved to work with him and because the hacking was enough reason to believe that our work in exposing the brutal regime was paying off. I was, however, still cautious and thus avoided replying to his email. I decided to monitor the developments in the country so that by the time I emailed him back, I would be sending him news items.

Elated by the developments and the assurance by the editor, I regained some sense of strength and confidence – fear was gone, and sense of safety restored.

I went about my normal business. From the cybercafé, I went to a tele-center opposite the *Daily Observer* offices. I called a few friends and asked them what was going on in the country, since I had been away in the village all weekend. They told me about the arrests of more people, some of whom I knew.

I then called my wife, Teddi Jallow, for a brief conversation. I missed her so much because she could not visit me the past weekend since I was away in the village. Since we married about two months earlier, we had been planning our own bride-welcoming ceremony either for that year or for the following year. She had seized the opportunity of her lunch break at school to visit the wife of one of my friends near her school. I narrated how colorful the bride-welcoming ceremony was and how all my friends asked after her. After I finished talking to Teddi, I stayed for a few more minutes in the telephone booth, thinking about the whole trouble in the media. Even though the *Freedom* newspaper editor's email had reassured me, I still felt feverish and cold. I still wore my sweater that even seemed not enough for me. I knew people would think I was crazy if I said I felt cold in the middle of such a sweltering day. My body also ached. I stood inside the booth, leaned my forehead against the wall while I placed my hand on the telephone handle. I came out, gave some money to the operator and walked away. Midway out of the tele-centre, just as I was about to cross the road into the *Daily Observer* premises, someone from the tele-centre ran after me and handed me some money that should have been my change. "Oh thank you. I forgot that I had some money left," I said, as I crossed the road.

About 2 p.m. that fateful Monday, the office receptionist opened the door to the computer room where I was. She told me to answer a telephone call. It was one Alhagie Mbye in London. I was surprised to get a call from him. He had been a senior reporter at *The Independent* newspaper a few years earlier, while I was a rookie reporter there. Since he left for the UK a few years earli- er, I had not had any contact with him.

"Hello!" I said.

"Who is that, Omar Bah?" He sounded nervous and he was literally scream- ing at the top of his voice.

"Yes, it's me."

"My brother, it's me Alhagie Mbye. Do you have a cell phone?" "Yes."

"Give me the number and move away from the public. I'll call you on your cell phone immediately and I want to talk to you about something very seri- ous."

I gave him my cell phone number. "Okay, bye," I said and put down the phone. I was charging my cell phone battery inside the computer room. I quickly unplugged the phone and rushed outside to the balcony in the shade of a mango tree. The cell phone rang.

"Omar Bah!"

"Yes? What's going on?"

He told me that I was in deep trouble, that the government hacker had initiated more trouble by succeeding in accessing the stories I had been filing for the *Freedom* newspaper. He said most of the articles I had emailed to the *Freedom* newspaper editor, had been circulated among Gambian online chat forums and that many people had already commented on my safety and security. He mentioned one Ebou Jallow, an associate of the dictator, as one of the people desperately circulating the said emails on the Internet. I could not figure out the whole thing. It was just too much for me. If the hacker accessed the emails he was talking about, that meant I had better start running away or face death – as those emails contained very revealing information about the dictatorship.

"One thing I have to tell you is that the government can kill you any moment. Leave that office immediately because if people like me in the UK can see this, it means the security officers must already be looking for you. Your name is there, with your email address. Please leave now!" He screamed, almost pleading, before putting down the phone.

That was one of the most terrifying moments in my life. I felt a chill run through the top to the bottom of my body. My body convulsed involuntarily. I started sweating profusely. My heart throbbed, while my head pounded, as if someone was repeatedly hitting me with a hammer. My legs buckled and I crumpled on the floor.

I had written many articles for the *Freedom* newspaper as its Banjul bureau chief. The prevailing censorship in the country was simply unbearable, so much so that some of us had taken to the *Freedom* newspaper as an alternative means of disseminating news that could liberate our people from the bondage of tyranny, poverty and misrule. Armed security men had attacked and burned down newspaper houses as well as the private residences of targeted journalists some of whom had even received death threats through anonymous letters. I had been in touch with my friend and colleague, Pa Nderry M'bai, who was living in exile in the USA. Sometimes he would call me, but in most cases, we would communicate through email, and we had always discussed the harassment and censorship in the Gambian media. Since he arrived in the USA, he had been very active in the campaign against the dictatorship, and the fight against media and human rights suppression in our country.

One night early in February 2006, on my way to visit a friend, as I was waiting for transport by the Bundung roadside in the city of Serrekunda, my cell phone rang. It was Pa Nderry. As soon as I picked the call, he triumphantly announced to me that he had launched an online newspaper named the *Freedom* newspaper and asked me whether I would work with him in his quest for independent and free journalism for our country. I agreed right away. He gave me the newspaper's email and website addresses and asked that I be his point man in The Gambia. I was excited at the prospects of exposing the murderous and corrupt government of President Yahya Jammeh.

I was delighted that such an important milestone had been made in the history of the Gambian media. The continued censorship and attacks on journalists was uncalled for. With the coming into being of the *Freedom* newspaper, we would be able to operate freely, and the government would not be able to do anything to stop us. I would have to use a pseudonym, a mere "Banjul Bureau Chief" being the main correspondent in Banjul among a host of numerous other anonymous identities. That was the only thing we could do to save our lives since we were riding on a breakthrough in the midst of an evil dictatorial regime. Therefore, it was only the editor in the US, Pa Nderry, who worked openly for the paper. I was working at the *Daily Observer* while simultaneously working for the *Freedom* newspaper, which gave me access to more information for the *Freedom* newspaper. Whenever stories that the *Daily Observer* management deemed seditious and not fit for publication came to my desk as news editor at the Daily Observer, I forwarded them to the *Freedom* newspaper. The government soon became concerned and suspicious about the growing popularity of the *Freedom* newspaper and called for the names of the journalists writing for the paper.

I had written many articles for *Freedom* newspaper, notably about The Gambia government's sinister support for separatist rebels from neighbouring Senegalese region of Casamance, including admitting their wounded into The Gambia's main hospital. I reported to the *Freedom* newspaper the torture of soldiers in detention and the breaking of their arms because the President questioned their loyalty, as well as the endless murder and secret burials of these by the government. I also discussed an alleged quarrel between the president and his mother over his maladministration of the country because of which she collapsed and was subsequently hospitalized for suspected high blood pressure. My other stories revealed the detention of government opponents, corruption and many other cases of administrative malpractice by the Jammeh regime.

Therefore, *Freedom* newspaper reached the Gambian readership with necessary, balanced, objective information routinely classified as criticism by the Jammeh rogue regime. Soon, the *Freedom* newspaper became very popular. That was because we gave the Gambian people what they needed to read and not what the government wanted them to read. Thousands of readers visited the website daily, far more than the readership of the physical tabloids in the country. On 21 March 2006, a group of soldiers was accused of attempting to overthrow the government of President Yahya Jammeh, and the mayhem and human destruction that followed was unimaginable. This was not the first time the president and his associates had accused citizens of attempts to overthrow his government. This latest accusation was just one of many monotonous public scares that the Gambian government had instilled in the psyche of the people. The government arrested scores of soldiers and civilians including lawyers and parliamentarians, as a result. These detainees suffered severe physical and mental torture involving both caning and electrocution at the bunkers of the deadly National Intelligence Agency (NIA). Government security agents murdered and buried a good number of them including security chiefs in unmarked mass graves.

The rest of the detainees were tortured and never allowed access to lawyers or arraigned in court. Paraded on national television, they were forced to confess publicly their involvement in the alleged coup attempt. After being in detention for so long, some of the soldiers and civilians appeared before a High Court judge. I was among the journalists who attended that court sitting. It was a very sad and emotional day seeing the families of the detainees break down in tears as they saw their loved ones in miserable physical condition. I saw an army captain, Bunja Darboe, whose arm, molded with some white stuff, hung with a string over his shoulder. In most of the faces of the detainees, one could visibly see the signs of torture. I sat at a little corner in the press gallery in the courtroom and thought to myself that the president indeed meant it when he continually threatened people that his prisons are "Africa's hell on Earth".

For me, a place where helpless people were subjected to such torture with their arms broken and some even killed with some reportedly buried alive, was much worse than 'Africa's hell on Earth'. I prayed and hoped that this brutality on my fellow citizens would end sooner than later.

It was upsetting to wake up every morning in The Gambia and think of Yahya Jammeh being President – someone who had fired thousands of Gambians from their jobs just for egoistic political reasons; continues to arrest and detain and kill Gambians for senseless reasons. The question that was in the minds of most Gambians was how the country could get rid of such a tyrant. At least I was glad that I was able to expose the atrocities in the *Freedom newspaper*.

As part of arrest and torture in the wake of the alleged coup attempt, security operatives rounded up all journalists at *The Independent* newspaper one morning and then briefly detained them at the paramilitary barracks, a short distance away from their office. They were released after a while but their General Manager, Madi Ceesay, and Editor-in-Chief, Musa Saidykhan, were not. In addition to the continued detention of the two bosses, state security agents forcibly shut down the newspaper. A few days after those horrible incidents, security agents pounced on a third journalist, Lamin Fatty, from the same newspaper.

During this crackdown on the media, I found myself in a very challenging situation. I happened to be the only member of the Gambia Press Union (GPU) executive who was in town. The President and Vice President of the Union were respectively Madi and Musa who were now in detention. The rest of the members were all out of the country or unreachable. Therefore, it fell on me to run up and down seeking their release on behálf of the GPU. International media rights organizations were contacting me constantly for updates on the media clampdown. At the same time, I kept updating the *Freedom* newspaper about the developments as they unfolded. I was now getting increasingly busy. The Voice of America (VOA) was also constantly contacting me for reports about the situation on the ground. In fact, a few people had already warned me to watch out because, according to them, the government was displeased with my reporting for the VOA.

The freed staff members of *The Independent* newspaper were also doing their own efforts to get the trio out of detention. From time to time, they and I would meet at some secure locations and update each other on our various efforts. In one of such meetings, I met with the deputy editor of the paper, Sulayman Makalo, who disclosed to me that the detainees were being seriously tortured. He said he learned from relatives of the detained journalists (who were now allowed to bring food to them at the NIA headquarters) that Musa even had open wounds on his face and arms. We both shared this exclusive with all the international organizations interested in the ordeals of the three journalists. I quickly informed the Gambia Media Support (GAMES) and a host of other organizations and concerned individuals outside the country. I had two older journalists, Sam Sarr and Swaebou Conateh, by my side helping and sometimes moving around with me from one place to another, for the release of our colleagues. At some point, the three of us went to the *Foroyaa* newspaper offices, where Sam was editor, and wrote a GPU press release demanding that the government release the three detained journalists. I distributed the press release to the media houses in the country. I did not give the *Daily Observer* and the Gambia Radio and Television Services (GRTS) copies because I knew they would not publish or broadcast it. Instead, after distributing the hard copies of the press release to the local media, I went to a cybercafé in Serrekunda, typed the press release and emailed it to the *Freedom* newspaper, which published it immediately.

The Committee to Protect Journalists (CPJ), an organization based in the U.S., sent a representative, Tidiane Sy, to investigate the detention of the journalists. He had contacted me before he came to Banjul and we worked together on his hotel accommodation and appointments with various officials and individuals. When he arrived, we kept going up and down the capital city, Banjul, in an effort to speak to security personnel. At the police headquarters, we waited for hours on end without seeing the people we set out to see. Worse still, we could not have a lawyer to represent the GPU. We both visited a lawyer whom we thought might help the GPU but she declined outright. The situation became increasingly desperate for us. When Tidiane completed his CPJ investigations, he left The Gambia with little, if any, accomplishment at all.

It took several weeks before the government finally released Madi and Musa, but kept the third journalist Lamin Fatty in detention. Sulayman Makalo told me that the authorities had freed my GPU executive colleagues. I immediately informed all the human rights organizations I was in touch with about the release of the two journalists.

I called both Madi and Musa and spoke to them. Madi particularly expressed thanks for my commitment, because he said he had learned about my specific efforts in getting them out of detention. I told both of them that I was honored to have played my part in securing their freedom and that I needed them to know and appreciate the big role Sam and Swaebou had played in their release. I also told them about Pap Saine, the co-proprietor of *The Point newspaper*, who even reportedly helped their families financially. In addition, I told them about the loyalty and steadfastness of their staff at *The Independent* newspaper.

A few days after their release, in early May 2006, Madi selected me to join him as a part of a two-man delegation to represent The Gambia at the West African Journalists' Association (WAJA) congress in Abidjan, the capital city of the Ivory Coast. That was going to be my first international activity and I was very honored to be part of it, especially when I was one of the youngest, if not the youngest, at the congress, and thus had a lot to learn from my well experienced colleagues in the sub-region. During the congress, both Madi and I expounded on the miserable case of the Gambian media by giving a catalogue of media rights violations in the country. I made many new friends among colleagues in the media from the various countries of the sub-region. A couple of media rights defenders who were not practising journalists per se, were also invited and I happened to get to meet and build close friendship with some of them especially those from neighbouring Senegal. A couple of them gave me their business cards and urged me to keep in touch. An older woman whose eloquence at the congress I admired so much gave me her business card as we waited for a flight back to Senegal at the airport in Abidjan and asked me in Wollof to keep in touch with her. I returned home, more fired up and more resolved to fight for press freedom in my country.

I knew the authorities were unhappy with me because of my role as both a journalist and a free expression activist in the country, but for them now to have irrefutable proof of what they see as my seditious writing, is a different kettle of fish altogether.

4

I was still at the balcony of the *Daily Observer* offices. I held the wall and managed to get up. I ran into the office. There were many people around. I stopped running lest they suspect I was among the *Freedom* newspaper's stringers and give me away to the authorities. As I walked past into the editorial office to pick my bag, Ramatu, the receptionist, followed me in.

"Omar, what's wrong?" She said. She had been watching me since I received the first call and suspected that I had not been my usual self.

"You...," I said with some hesitation. "You don't know.... I'll talk to you later." I picked up my bag and rushed out of the editorial room. I stopped. For some inexplicable reasons, I went into the computer room where someone saw the bag and suspected I was heading out of the office.

"I hope you will be back soon? Come back soon because we have to take the paper to print soon, so that we will not spend the night here again," the person said.

"I'll be back soon," I said.

Deep in my heart, however, I knew I would not be back soon. I wished the person knew. As a farewell gesture to my colleagues in the computer room, I pulled out a fifty-dalasi note from my back pocket and gave the people in computer room to buy soft drinks. As they celebrated the gift, I walked out. I ran across the road in between cars. My head ached and my legs trembled. Because I was inattentive to the traffic, a car nearly hit me. The driver swerved off the road and screeched to a halt. That attracted some onlookers. Upset by my inattention and apparent indifference, the driver verbally abused me repeatedly, but I continued on. When I got on the other side of the road to wait for commercial transport, I was alert and roved my eyes in every direction just in case some- one suspicious approached. I saw the Managing Director of the Daily Observ- er, Dr Saja Taal, alight from his car and stride towards the office building. He was a strong ally of the dictator and was responsible for most of the censorship of my work as a journalist at the newspaper. I walked a little farther towards the trunk of a huge tree nearby, just to avoid him because my gut reaction was that he was looking for me over the *Freedom* newspaper saga.

I had always been very cautious during my latter days at the Daily Observer, when two allies of the dictator Mam Sait Ceesay and Saja Taal were brought in as editor-in-chief and as managing director respectively. They introduced high level of government intrusion, censorship and threats. The country was headed for a presidential election in 2006 and it was evident that with the ex- cessive intrusion and censorship of the editorial independence of the newspa- per, tougher times lay ahead. It was also evident that the dictatorship was poised to do anything to remain in power and one way in which to do that was to muscle the press and covertly and overtly use the Daily Observer, the coun- try's biggest paper, as a propaganda tool.

Stringent pro-government editorial policies were imposed in October 2005 when Saja Taal and Mam Sait Ceesay (who doubled as press officer at the Office of the President) came to the newspaper. Their policies were purposely intended to appease the dictator and the ruling party regardless of the general readership preference. They made it categorically clear that nothing critical of the president and his party was to be published in the paper yet they orchestrat- ed regular attacks and insults on opponents of the ruling party.

In my capacity as news editor, I always made clear my concern for the credi- bility of the paper. Shortly after the imposition of the groveling Taal-Ceesay editorial policies, the sales of the paper dropped, proving my point. The new bosses became increasingly uncomfortable with the arguments and suggestions that I presented at Senior Management Team meetings. Merely because of my persistence on the need for balanced reporting, the managing director promptly branded me an opposition element, threatening me with sacking and imprison- ment. In general, journalists in the country were suffering under the dictator. The situation that hitherto used to be arrest, torture, and closure of media houses now had a new element added to it–assassination. For instance, on the night of Thursday December 16, 2004, suspected agents of the state shot and killed Deyda Hydara, the editor of *The Point newspaper*, as he drove past a paramilitary barracks. Two of his female staff whom he was driving home, sustained serious injuries. Up until now, his murder remains unsolved. A few days after the murder, I joined some of my colleagues at Radio 1 FM to voice our disgust over the killing and announced our plan to embark on a peaceful march.

The march went on with journalists wearing shirts bearing the photo of our colleague with the slogan: "Who killed Deyda Hydara?" The protest march did not go down well with the powers that be because they refused us to gather at the venue where we initially intended to converge. Moreover, they disallowed the public to join the journalists in the protest march. As we marched through the streets of Banjul heading to the police headquarters and later, the Ministry of the Interior, hundreds of heavily armed soldiers, some masked, lined up the entire city. But the level of moral support we received from onlookers – people lining the side streets sobbing – clearly shows that the Gambian people were fed up with the Jammeh government and its brutal tactics. As soon as we finished the march, the soldiers forced us to disperse immediately. The day did not end without more chaos in the country—the head of the military in the country was sacked shortly after we dispersed from the march, for reasons that might not have been unconnected with our street protest. There were speculations that he was sacked because he refused to comply with the president's order to shoot at us as we marched along the streets of Banjul.

Following that brutal murder, the journalists in the country went on a news blackout—neither publishing newspapers nor broadcasting on radio—for a whole week. It was meant to reinforce our collective stance against the growing impunity in the country. In fact, on the morning following the murder, the dictator and hundreds of his supporters partied on the beach behind the State House. The preparation for the strike was prompt and perfectly executed. On the Sunday morning that followed the assassination, my phone rang and it was my editor-in-chief, Ndey Tapha Sosseh, on the line. She said she wanted me in the office as soon as possible because she needed me to be there while she talked about the issue of laying down tools for the whole week. I rushed out of my apartment and headed to the office. My editor-in-chief kept calling me repeatedly and urged me to rush over to the office because she considered my presence crucial at the meeting she was about to convene at the office. I cannot remember how many times she called before I reached the *Daily Observer* offices. By the time I got there, most of my colleagues had been waiting. As soon as I entered the venue of the meeting, the editor-in-chief, addressed everyone, disclosing that she had gathered everyone so that she would take a decision on a week-long media blackout—but that before taking such a momentous decision, she needed to know everybody's standpoint. We all told her to go ahead with the decision because we were all behind her. Then we all took our belongings and marched out of the office, officially starting the strike.

In reprisal for initiating the strike, my editor-in-chief was summarily dismissed. That was yet another confirmation of who the true owner of the *Daily Observer* is—the name of a businessman appeared on the paper as the owner, but government officials were often affirming that the businessman was simply a front for the president who was the real owner of the paper. The president from all indications owned the paper because he dictated what happened there. So if my editor-in-chief was fired merely for seeking justice for a murdered colleague, the person who fired her must have been very well offended by her action.

A few months after the sacking of the editor-in-chief, the managing director, Sheriff Bojang, also left the company. That was another blow to the independence of the newspaper because he had run a fairly balanced editorial policy. Bojang's style sustained the credibility of the Daily Observer, by being independent and moderate.

Since the killing of Deyda, fear and suspicion of the security forces had dominated the media. Several journalists decided to quit the profession due to family pressure or flee the country for fear for their lives. The rest, like me, who chose to remain in the profession, were under stiff family pressure to quit though we were able to resist. Every journalist was expecting any time to be the next casualty of the tyrant's scorched earth policy.

Sometime in 2005, I was elected First Assistant Secretary General of the Gambia Press Union (GPU), the main journalist organization in the country. Later, when the secretary general was out of the country, the Union elevated me to her position. That further placed me in greater danger and exposure. However, I was proud to be in that new executive of the union under the leadership of veteran journalist Madi Ceesay.

In December 2005, the GPU executive which I was part of, organized a huge international conference in the country to commemorate the first anniversary of the assassination of Deyda Hydara. Colleagues from around the continent and other parts of the world converged to express the need for investigation into the assassination and for a free press in the country. As expected, the event did not go without hurdles. Participants from some international organisations, particularly those from Reporters Without Borders, were denied visas to enter the country. Nevertheless, the worst trouble from the government came when, towards the end of the conference, we visited the spot of the assassination for the purpose of laying a wreath and praying for our departed colleague. The government sent trucks full of paramilitary officers who stopped us midway. Security agents attacked and beat some journalists who had reached the scene earlier. One of them, Ramatoulie Charreh, a female reporter at the Daily Observer, was hospitalized as a result. After our fruitless attempt to lay the wreaths, we left the scene to converge at the Hydara family home for final prayer and speeches by the elders and conference participants.

This incident caused great confusion at the Daily Observer. The managing director, Saja Taal, sacked Ramatoulie Charreh. His reason was that she should not have allowed herself to have a confrontation with "national security". Dr Taal had also written and published an editorial sullying the memory of the late Deyda Hydara whom he accused of having been a spy for neighbouring Senegal among a host of other lies. The atmosphere was tense at the Daily Observer. Even the editor-in-chief, Mam Sait Ceesay, complained about that ridiculous editorial. His comments, however, fell on deaf ears.

When Ramatoulie told me about her sacking, I was angry because I know as a journalist, your employers should always stand by you whenever you are in trouble, and not throw you to the wolves. I told her that she was not going anywhere. I made it clear to the managing director that if he didn't rescind his decision of firing the journalist, I was going to lead a mass resignation at the office. At the end, the managing director backed down and rescinded his decision. But just few days after that, Ramatoulie called me aside and spoke to me; she thanked me for what she saw as my honesty and principle but said she could not work at the *Daily Observer* any more, as according to her, she had decided with her family that she would quit the job. She wrote a resignation letter which she even showed me. I thanked her for her trust in me before she tendered her resignation letter to the managing director. I did not object to her idea about resigning because I supported her reasons as her news editor.

However, I was yet to see the last of Saja Taal's capricious nature. One early morning, a phone call interrupted my sleep. It was Ousman Darboe. He told me that the managing director had fired him for granting an interview to Radio France International on the day of the attack by security personnel, and for wearing a T-shirt bearing the picture of the late Deyda Hydara to the *Daily Observer* offices. At first, I thought he was joking and asked him not to disrupt my sleep with his silly jokes. He however insisted that he was dead serious, bleating that the managing director had asked him to leave the *Daily Observer* premises immediately. To drive home his point, he said he was holding his dismissal letter right in his hands, as we spoke. That jolted me out of my complacency and I asked him to disregard the managing director's directive until I got to the office. He told me it was impossible for him to stay a little longer within the premises because the managing director was keeping a close tab on him. I coaxed him into finding a way of waiting for me.

"Please wait for me," I said. "You are not going alone. I am going to resign myself if he does not change his decision. Go to the marketing office. It is very secluded there. Tell them I asked you to wait for me there and that nobody else should know about your presence there. Please do me that favor. Okay?" He agreed.

I rose from my bed and was out of my apartment in a matter of minutes. When I reached the office, I went straight to the marketing section. I yanked the dismissal letter from Ousman Darboe and skimped through it. I could tell from his body language that he was not keen on what I was doing. All he wanted was for me to let him go away from the pain and tragedy that the managing director symbolized. I empathized with him. Nevertheless, I made it clear to him that, as news editor, I would not allow a bunch of political sycophants and stooges to ride roughshod over my reporters–that deciding to quit the job would be one's prerogative but to be dismissed for political consideration was a different matter altogether. With the letter in my hand, I went with Ousman Darboe and some reporters to the managing director's office and told him to change his decision. It seemed he was waiting for me to make my threat of a mass resignation once again. He made a series of frivolous complaints against the reporter, but finally reversed his decision. The reporter got his job back.

One of the most ridiculous things that the new management of the paper did was its open censorship, accompanied with threats against independent-minded reporters. As the paper was being prepared for print each night, both the managing director and editor- in-chief would be present to substitute material they deemed dissident to the president and his government with advertisements as well as articles and commentaries denigrating opponents of the regime. What made that practice worse was the fact that some officials from the Office of the President and Ministry of Information sometimes joined the managing director and editor-in-chief in the farce of making the paper politically correct.

One of the main preoccupations of the new management was also to censor my interview column, *"Bantaba."* Management insisted I feature only government and ruling party officials whom I should ask 'favourable' questions. I promptly stopped the column because I had always seen myself as a professional journalist, not a political apparatchik.

There were no signs that the hostility towards journalists and independent press at the *Daily Observer* would stop any time soon. I had been thinking a lot about my future there. At some point, I decided that it was time for me to resign and move on with my life. I wrote a resignation letter and gave it to the deputy managing director, Andrew Dacosta whom, when he received my resignation letter, called me to a quiet place—at the balcony, in the shade of the mango tree—and asked what work I was going to do after my disengagement from the Daily Observer. I told him I could no longer take the political interference in the newspaper and wanted out. In his usual cool and calm manner, he advised me to give the "new management a chance" and see what would happen.

I joined a commercial transport and headed to the city center of Serrekunda, where I paid for a thirty-minute usage at a cybercafé and sat before a computer in the corner of the room. The place where I sat was so secluded that I walked in almost unnoticed. I tried to enter the Gambia Post chat forum, but I could not because I needed to enter a membership password. I was not a member of that forum and had never visited it before. I was nervous, as I tried to keep an eye on anyone entering the cybercafé and at the same time struggling to enter the site to see what my colleague from the UK was talking about. I was still wearing the sweater that I wore in the morning. I was sweating profusely until my clothes were completely wet. Suddenly, a call came in.

"Omar Bah, it's me Alhagie Mbye calling you from London again. Have you seen your emails to the *Freedom* newspaper that the hacker accessed, that Ebou Jallow exposed at the Gambia Post?"

The same caller had alerted me earlier.

"No. I'm trying but I can't enter the site," I said.

He then told me how to enter the site, even as a non-member.

When I told him I had already accessed it, he said, "I will let you go through it and see how much danger you are in. Be very careful, my brother, okay?" When I got access to the Gambia Post online chat forum, I saw emails, as I had sent them to the *Freedom* newspaper—about killings, torture, corruption and a host of administrative malpractices of the regime—in full view. People were already commenting on the development, with some, including *Freedom* newspaper editor Pa Nderry M'bai, damning a certain associate of the dictator, one Ebou Jallow, for forwarding the hacked material (if he was not the actual hacker) and thus putting me in harm's way. Ebou, who posted a good number of my email exchanges with the *Freedom* newspaper Pa Nderry, did not explain from where and how he got the emails. However, it was easy to suspect that he either was the hacker or was being used by the dictator to spread the hacked material in order to put me in more danger.

Below is his introductory statement as he posted the hacked material, in which he suggested that my work as a journalist is a criminal act, rather than an act in the defense of press freedom:

Ladies and Gentlemen,
Here is Pa Nderry M'bai at his best goading Gambian journalists and online subscribers in Banjul to spread innuendoes, churn sedition and slander honorable Gambian citizens. Is this an exercise of

press freedom or blatant criminal activity by a twisted mind un-hinged....? You be the judge.

E.

The email on top of the list of the hacked material was one that I had sent to the *Freedom* Editor. In it, I discussed a variety of things.

Hi,

Boy it was great to receive your mail. It is true, let us keep in touch. You were smart not to mention my identity but (be) rest assured I will keep you posted with latest on the ground. Just keep my identity concealed or call me BARU.

Yes, James is right. It was good you spoke to him to give him more encouraging words about me. I'm sure with your backing, they will have more confidence in me. Well, so far, he has been encouraging me (a) lot and has also been asking me to keep up the good work as according to him, I have been doing a good job since they started contacting me after the coup. He is very impressed and people like Lamin Cham are also encouraging me a lot. So I am pretty sure with the additional involvement of people like you, everything will work well.

I would like you also to guide me on how to go about everything as regards programs and reportage... you name them. Hope to hear from you soon on that.

Otherwise, the breaking news in The Gambia is that Speaker Sheriff Dibba has been arrested at 2am Thursday. Where he is now and the reason(s) for his arrest are yet to be known. You can develop that.

Greetings, Omar Bah

Then, another email in which I reported about the relocation of the residence of the president's mother due to security threats:

Hi Pa,

Jammeh's mother moved following death threats.

The Gambia is a very insecure place these days. Jammeh's mother who was living in Cape Point Bakau all the while, an opposition stronghold, has suddenly been moved to a highly secured place in Kotu.

The decision which is a top security secret in the country was disclosed to me by a woman who is for us (the *Freedom* Newspaper) and is always in the company of the President's mother. These are facts that, when released by this paper, Jammeh will have a hard knock on his head!

According to undisputable sources, the whole problem started when the coup theory emerged and innocent and helpless Gambians were arrested and killed by this mad President. Some unidentified people, in the form of letters and subversive messages, glaringly threatened the president's mother, Asombi Bojang, with death threats lest her son stopped the madness in the country.

Then while the mother was in Foni Bwiam for a naming ceremony this week, Jammeh transferred all her things to a new place in Kotu. From Bwiam, she was then driven straight to her new place. She was said to not like that place as according to her, it is not as luxurious as where she used to be, but the son who has no respect, threatened to return her to Foni (where she does not like), if she does not accept. Today, that place is so highly secured just as State House.

According to our sources, the place is a 4 storey building situated near the residence of the Taiwanese ambassador. This move is calculated so that both the ambassador and the President's mother can be heavily secured simultaneously because they share the same neighbourhood now.

However, residents in Bakau are now scared of moving around the former residence of Asombi Bojang as they fear to be suspected as the ones giving out threats and, as usual, accused of treason. There is a stiff surveillance mounted around the vicinity of her former residence just to apprehend suspects.

This is a sad insecurity situation for our country. The man is just mad now and is so scared now.

Meanwhile, the president has reinstated his mother's personal nurse who was sacked for fear that he was a spy. But when the president realised that that was a lie emanating from himself, he accepted his mother's call to bring back the nurse.

And yet there was another very revealing email in which I talked about the government-censored newspaper, *Daily Observer*, where I worked, and another story about the president's mother:

Boy,

Here is a piece I returned since Sunday. I just had to settle one or two things so I could not reply my mails. But I am intact, just frustrated working in this place. If I had another place, I would really quit this shit of a place. Below is a piece for you:

Jammeh's mother hospitalised by Our Banjul Bureau Chief

Reports reaching the *Freedom* Newspaper have revealed that Asombi Bojang, the mother of Gambian president, Yahya Jammeh, is currently being hospitalised at the Intensive Care unit of the Royal Victoria Teaching Hospital (RVTH).

Reports suggest that the president's mother has been at the hospital since Tuesday on a very threatening sickness. According to sources close to her, the ailment arose following the abortive March 21 coup. She is said to have develop[ed] fear in her when her son, the president, started treating Gambians badly and "upon realisation of the possible consequences to her son, she began to advise him not to do any of the bad things he is doing, like killings, threats, witch-hunts, etc. She must have sensed her son's (imminent) downfall." The *Freedom* Newspaper has learnt that following that advice, the president refused to take heed and even warned his mother to put her mouth out of STATE MATTERS. He is reported to have said that he would not allow his mother to interfere in what he is doing.

Following the intense frustration, Asombi Bojang reportedly collapsed on Tuesday morning and is still at the RVTH under intensive care. We have learned that plans are underway to fly her abroad for urgent treatment.

Currently, heavily armed soldiers are guarding the hospital, especially at nights, and President Jammeh visits there at odd hours unexpectedly.

Then there was an email from the *Freedom* newspaper editor:

Thanks boy for the good piece. You are part of the *Freedom* newspaper and we count on you. We will try to wire you some money later on. Once the money is wired, I will notify you. Keep up the good work.

I understand your frustrations at the Obs but keep the faith. Stay in touch with *Freedom*. Don't underestimate your contributions. It will pay off. This paper is widely read. Keep your identity strictly confidential. We will do whatever it takes to protect you. Feel free to send stories at any time.

As time goes on, I will give you editorial rights so that you can post stories from The Gambia. You do not need to email me your stories. It is easy. I will show you how to do it. You are a true brother and I trust you. Take it easy and regards to wife. Later.

NB: Keep us posted about Jammeh's mum story and the by-elections....

Cheers, Pa Nderry

I did send more stories:

Hi Boy, Two pieces

Jammeh's mother discharged

Asombi Bojang, the mother of President Yahya Jammeh of The Gambia, has been discharged from the Royal Victoria Teaching Hospital (RVTH) after hav ing been admitted there for at least a week.

The president's mother collapsed from a strange sickness on Tuesday 8th May and was immediately rushed to the hospital. She was reportedly in coma for few days but recovered just when plans were underway to fly her out of The Gambia for better medical attention.

A source of the *Freedom* newspaper who is a close relative of the President's mother, visited her on Sunday and said that she (Asombi) is still in bad shape. She however expressed hope that things improve.

Asombi Bojang is back at her new Kotu villa, a former residence of disgraced majority leader, Baba Jobe.

Captain Bunja Darboe's arm broken, face swollen

Accused person Number 1, in the so-called treason case of the March 21 attempted coup, Captain Bunja Darboe, last Wednesday appeared before the High Court presided over by Justice Mrs SM Monageng. (He had) both a broken arm (which was molded with white material and hung over his neck) and a seriously swollen face.

Drama unfolded when the 16 of the accused persons arrived in court [and] hundreds of people started to cry when they saw the state in which Bunja was. It is his left arm, with which he writes, that is broken. Bunja is said to be hated by the Chiakas (the president's torturers) as he is seen as an intellectual, and therefore, want to eliminate him.

More on this soon

After reading through all these emails, I was confused and did not know what to do. I had written scores more stories for the *Freedom* newspaper, and I could not imagine how much more information the dictator or Ebou Jallow still had. Whatever else they still had, I was convinced, given the damning stories I had filed for the paper, that Jammeh's goons would kill me in cold blood if they laid their hands on me.

By now, I was so terrified that I was afraid to leave the cybercafé. I kept extending my usage time so that I could remain inside. Mam Sait Ceesay, my editor-in-chief at the Daily Observer, kept calling me and asking for my whereabouts, demanding that I return to the office to work. Each time he called, I responded that I was having a meeting somewhere in town and that I would return later. Nevertheless, he kept calling over and over demanding I tell him where I was. Finally, I stopped answering his calls. Several other people I knew were also calling me. I picked up some calls, while I ignored others. Some of them were security agents, who even identified themselves as such. Moreover, the security agents who called would not state their names but would just order me to tell them where I was, or report to the nearest state security center, warning that if I refused to do so, I would face dire consequences. I was so worried and confused about everything that I contemplated surrendering myself to the nearest police station and then face the consequences finally.

I did not know how to avoid receiving the calls from the security agents because when they called, their numbers would not appear on the screen of my cell phone, just like the calls from my friends in the UK. Because I did not want to miss the calls from my friends, I answered any anonymous call I received. Unaware of my own dilemma, the security agents kept calling and threatening me. Just then, another call with a hidden number came in.

"Hello."

"Yes, who is this?" I said.

"It's me, Sheriff Bojang Junior."

He is a journalist and relative of my one-time managing director who happened to have the same name too. He had been living in the UK for some years now. Until recently, I had worked with him on a cultural magazine called *W aato*.

"But Omar are you okay?" He said in a slight British accent. His voice was low and nervous.

"No, I'm not okay," I said.

He asked me if I had seen the exposure of my stories against the dictator, and I told him that I was in fact at a cybercafé staring at the stories.

"So Omar what are you going to do now?" His voice sounded melancholic. He confessed to me that before dialing my cell phone number, he thought I was already dead, and was just gambling – he could not believe that I was indeed alive and was speaking with him. "Omar, this man (the president) is very angry. He will harm you if he gets hold of you."

"I don't know what to do. I definitely do not know. I am just sitting here. I don't know," I said. My voice quaked and I felt like crying. My head felt like lead—it ached so much that my vision blurred. Sheriff Bojang Junior also sounded increasingly worried. He suggested I rush out of the cybercafé and seek refuge at the U.S. embassy or at the British high commission. He cajoled me to do his bidding immediately.

I gave him my word and then called an acquaintance that I told what was going on. He could not believe what I had just said. As he was sympathizing and thinking of what he could do to help me, I told him I could no longer continue the conversation and then hung up on him. Then I called Ousman Darboe.

"Hello, Ousman."

"Omar, is everything okay with you?" He must have sensed from my trembling voice that I was in some sort of trouble.

"No. Something serious is going on. But...." "What is it? Are you safe?"

"No, Ousman. But..., I will call you later, okay, and bye." I ended the call. I felt as though the whole world was crumbling on me and wished the ground would break open and swallow me up and thus end this misery. I was trembling all over with fear and despair.

Inexplicably, I felt safe within the confines of the cybercafé. At that point, I had been inside the cybercafé for hours. Abruptly, power went off. The woman running the cybercafé pleaded with the customers to wait patiently while she put on her stand-by generator. When she did, she came back inside and asked me to pull some switches that were overhead where I was sitting. I rose and pulled something.

Fire sparkled. People ran helter-skelter outside the cafe. At the tiny door of the cybercafé, most of the customers managed to jostle their way outside. Unlike the other customers, I could not escape because the cybercafé operator pulled my shirt with one hand and used the other to pummel my head, while she heaped invective on me. Amidst this stampede, someone rushed to the switch and returned it to its original position, and thus averted the fire. Then he switched the right one on. The computers came on again and calm reigned. The stampede stopped, and the woman stopped hitting me. The customers waited outside while she made sure everything was okay. The man who averted the fire, also a customer, asked her to leave me alone as there was no damage done. She called the customers to come back. I regained my seat and said nothing. Outside in the street, there were dozens of onlookers already. I was more concerned about the attention the spark of fire and the woman's assault could bring to me. I did not want the customers inside the cybercafé, or the onlookers outside to notice me. Therefore, I just focused on my computer screen to avoid people seeing my face.

The woman kept staring at me from where she sat. I was not thinking about her attack. I had more serious things to worry about. To me my whole life was like a dream at that moment. Sometimes, I would look to my sides and outside to see whether I was not dreaming. After some time, the woman walked up to me and said in a Sierra Leonean accent, "My broda, I'm sorry, okay? Please forgive me in the name of Jesus, for what I've done."

I nodded my head and waved my right hand in acknowledgement, as I answered an incoming call. It was somebody from my office at the *Daily Observer* who was calling.

"Omar Bah, where are you? I know you know who is speaking. Don't mention my name," said the caller. "I'm somewhere."

"I am calling you from a tele-center so that no one will know that I called you. Omar, Please, I beg you…, do not come to the office right now. Whatever you might have done must be very serious. The soldiers are all over with guns looking for you. They are searching everywhere in the office. Moreover, I do not advise you to go to your apartment right now. Please don't tell anybody that I spoke to you, okay," he said and then ended the call.

Another colleague called to give me the information of armed security presence around the office. Then the calls kept coming. I refused to pick them. I could not talk. I could not even think. I pressed my head with my two hands in an effort to ease the pain. Apart from occasions when I had malaria, there was no other time my head ached me so seriously like that. I pulled the mini tape player from my bag and played Fula violin music to see if it would ease my worries. It did not make any difference and it even seemed as if I was not hearing anything. I pulled the headphones, switched off the tape and kept it back inside my bag. I dialed the number of Ebrima Baldeh.

"Hello, boy," he said when he received my call.

"Boy. Please come right now. You know the cybercafé near the Senegambia garage where we sometimes go."

"Yes!"

"I'm there. Please meet me there immediately."

"But..., boy..., boy, please tell me what's going on." He sounded agitated.

"Just come right now. I'll talk to you when you arrive," I said while I pressed a button on my cell phone to end the call.

Before my friend arrived, I received another call. It showed no number. I was worried because it could be the same security agents calling to threaten me yet again. I hesitated for a while before picking it up. However, it was my friend Sheriff Bojang Junior calling from London again.

"Omar!"

"Yes!"

"Omar, where are you? Are you at one of these embassies we discussed earlier?"

"No. But I'm about to go."

"Omar, I have been thinking about this since we discussed it. I do not think you should go to the embassies. The government security might get you while you are heading to the embassies. I am suggesting that you leave the country right away. Do not go to your house. You either sleep with a friend you trust until morning then you leave the country or try and leave right now." He was speaking very fast, as if someone was chasing after him, and his voice was loud and shaky. After he finished speaking, there was a lull as I was silent for a while.

"I'll do that. I'll leave right now, this night." I said.

Sheriff was with a friend at the time he was calling me, one Yankuba Dabo, who took the phone and spoke to me. He reiterated what Sheriff had just said, urging me to do my utmost to leave The Gambia, for my own good. He told me he was a fan of my one-on- one interviews and expressed how devastated he and his friend were at that moment. I promised him too that I would do exactly that. He returned the phone to Sheriff who further pleaded that I rush out of the country immediately.

Ebrima Baldeh who I had called and requested that he meet me at the cybercafé had arrived and was standing near me when I was speaking on the phone. After my conversation with Sheriff, I briefly explained to Ebrima Baldeh (who was already familiar with the story) about what was going on. I also showed him the emails that the hackers had posted online.

5

When I checked my time, I had spent almost the whole day at the cybercafé. The sun had now grown into a huge orange ball, hanging far down the horizon. It silhouetted the buildings in the clustered city so much, so that the whole city suddenly became dusky.

Ebrima Baldeh advised me to escape right away. We walked out of the cybercafé and onto a narrow street. As we walked side by side to a nearby road intersection where we would part ways, he would occasionally stop, attempt to say something, but then walk on. Neither of us said anything—aside from occasional stares at each other—we mostly looked down as we walked. I had to look down to avoid someone spotting my face. For my acquaintance, I soon realized that the reason why he was looking down as he walked was that he was sobbing profusely. Tears were rolling down his cheeks, and mucus gliding down his nostrils. His sniffles were so loud that anyone nearby could hear. My head was very heavy. I could hardly breathe. I tried to cry, but tears could not come out of my eyes. I broke the silence.

"Boy, if you cry like this, you will arouse the attention of the people and then I will be caught."

"Boy...," he said and then stopped. More tears rolled down his cheeks. His neck was all wet with tears.

I stopped talking to him. When we reached the junction, near Aishamari Cinema, we stood in the middle of the crowded road. It was the rush hour. In our culture, when a person is bidding farewell while embarking on a long journey in which you do not know when you will see each other again, you shake their left hands. That is the only time people will shake with their left hands. According to our lore, it is an implied prayer for the two of you to see each other soon again. That was how it was for my friend and me. We stretched out our left arms and shook hands. He could not control his emotions. More tears rolled. He was now crying aloud.

"Bye, Boy …. We will never see each other in life again," I said. He cried even louder as I said that.

"Please take care of Teddi for me," I said, referring to my wife.

However, before leaving, I remembered one more thing—my passport and school diplomas. I would need them wherever I would be in the world. That meant I had to rush to my apartment and quickly get those things before leaving the country. I did a quick search in my bag. Luckily, my passport was inside my bag. It had been there since I returned from my first international conference in the Ivory Coast some three weeks earlier. Now, my school diplomas were the only things I would worry about. When I told Ebrima Baldeh that I wanted to rush to my apartment to get them, he thought I had gone mad, as according to him, doing so would be like embarking on a suicide mission.

"But when the soldiers search my apartment, it is very likely that they will destroy those important documents, and I will never get them again," I told my friend.

"Boy…, leave this country and go. These soldiers may already be at your apartment waiting for you. Do not go near there. Your life is more important at the moment," he said.

Silence.

The two of us were still shaking each other's hand. After a while, Ebrima Baldeh ended it all, surprisingly without emotion.

"Boy, go. Go, go!"

He released my hand.

I almost fell to the ground. My body seemed much heavier than it used to be. My legs could not carry it. Somehow, I regained my balance.

Ebrima Baldeh walked westwards; I headed eastwards. We kept looking backwards and waving at each other until we both disappeared into the rush hour crowds. I started running. It was getting dark and the lights were not so bright. I ran as fast as I could. It was normal as there were so many people running up and down the road too—a motley crowd of wheelbarrow pushers, hawkers, pedestrians, and commuters. It was therefore easy for me to run without stand- ing out.

As I passed by the Serrekunda Police Station, I made sure I was on the other side of the road so that the crowd could block my visibility. I kept running until I reached the car park where I would pick a public transport heading to the capital city, Banjul. For some people who were attempting to escape from

38

the country, they would just have escaped through the south of the country and then into neighboring Senegal. However, I was brought up in the north of the country and would not risk trying to escape through a border that I was not quite familiar with, as I am with that of the north. I therefore decided to use the place I knew better. I joined a fourteen-seater commercial transport van heading to the capital. I took a seat at the back of the van, as it sped away.

Midway inside the city of Serrekunda, we got caught in a traffic jam, which delayed us for a while. The police were redirecting traffic for reasons I did not know. I was very worried that they were searching cars. Fortunately, they were not. Then the car reached the outskirts of Serrekunda city heading to Banjul. It slowed down. It was surprising there was traffic jam even on the highway. That was not normal. I only saw that happen once, when there was an attempted coup in the country. The vehicle was now in a line of hundreds of vehicles moving at a snail's pace and most of the time, stopping for a long while before inching forward again.

The prolonged delay scared me to death. My thoughts kept going back and forth, thinking about my family; my friends; and all I could remember in my short life of twenty-six years. I thought by allowing myself to wallow in such thoughts, I would be able to dispel my worries and stay calm. Yet, the premonition of imminent death that plagued me refused to go away.

The conductor of the commercial van asked for fares, interrupting my cogitation. I gave him a ten-dalasi note and he returned a change of four dalasis in coins. As I held the coins in my hand and looked out to see how far the vehicle had gone, I sensed danger. We were close to the Denton Bridge connecting the island of Banjul with the rest of the country, and there were hundreds of armed soldiers, police and paramilitary personnel wielding AK-47 guns. I panicked, and slid the window near me to get out of the vehicle so that I could vanish into the thickness of the mangroves.

However, as I was about to jump out, I noticed some movement; there were so many soldiers hiding within those shrubs, some of them lying down belly-wise, pointing their guns in the direction of the road. I closed the window slowly and sat back on my seat. I trembled hard and sweated profusely. On the back row where I sat, there was a woman sitting next to me. Throughout the journey, she had been fiddling with the hand of a guy who was sitting on the same row. My behaviour caught her attention. She released his hand and stared at me in bewilderment.

The driver of the vehicle was on the phone, apparently finding out from one of his colleagues what was going on up ahead in the traffic. When he finished talking, several people in the vehicle asked him simultaneously about what news he got.

"They are looking for somebody," he said in the Mandinka language.

Someone said it might be a coup and lamented that if she had known she would have remained indoors, tending her family. Everyone in the vehicle started praying so that no shootout would occur until we passed. I panicked further knowing I was now in my final minutes of life. I pulled the hand of the woman sitting next to me and gave her the four coins of money that the conductor had returned to me.

"What is this for?" She asked, in apparent awe. "Please pray for me. Pray for me...." My voice broke.

She turned toward me and kept praying for me. There was a sudden huge bang on the vehicle, and when I looked out, a soldier was standing in front, hopping, and displaying superabundant energy and arrogance. He was hitting the front of the vehicle with his gun butt and stamping it with his boots for it to come to a complete stop.

I could not think any more; my eyes could not see, and they hurt so much that it seemed as if one had sprayed pepper in them. I kept blinking fast; my hands were useless and so I dropped my handbag and clasped my hands in between my legs. The van rolled forward and then abruptly stopped bumping every- body against his or her seat. On both sides of the highway, other soldiers were apparently doing the same thing with other cars, while many more stood guards with guns pointed in the direction of the vehicles.

The conductor opened the door for the soldier to point his torch light and gun inside the car. The soldier banged repeatedly, while yelling and screaming that everyone should get their identification cards ready before he reached them. He did not enter the vehicle but just poked his head in as he looked at everybody's identification documents and pointed his gun and torch light at them. As everyone was busy looking for their documents in their wallets and bags, I just sat down doing nothing—my hands still clasped in between my legs, while I shivered and sweated profusely. The soldier was arrogant, shouting at anyone he turned to, and swearing at him or her for wasting his time.

When he was done with the woman sitting near me, it was my turn now— the last passenger. I did something different from what everyone had done. I knew at that moment that my time was over and thus did not have to show any document to warrant him shoot inside the vehicle and possibly even kill other passengers if he should shoot at me. Now, with a gun pointed at me, a torch light flashing into my face, I stood up and raised my arms up in surrender.

The soldier almost slipped from where he rested his foot when he saw me. I was awestruck too when I saw the person who was to kill me in a matter of seconds. I could not believe my eyes. It seemed he could not believe his either. We just kept staring at each other. His gun and torch light were no longer pointing at me. His lower jaw dropped, and he was visibly panic-stricken and shaken, but his eyes still bored into mine. "Omar B...!" He said, almost pronouncing my last name too.

I remembered him as an acquaintance from some years back. I did not say anything. I was still standing, with my arms up in the air.

It looked as though he was thinking fast. He tilted his head sideways repeatedly. Suddenly, he screamed at the driver.

"Move! Move! Move!"

He kicked our van and banged it with his gun butt, as he ran to another car to search. Our driver revved the engine and sped at an alarming speed, causing me to fall back on my seat. All the passengers then turned to me, asking a barrage of questions simultaneously: *A re you the one they are looking for? Who are you? What have you done? What is going on?*

I did not know what to say or do. I felt like I had just resurrected from the dead. "Pray for me," I said.

Then they stopped pestering me with questions and concentrated on praying for me. All the other passengers were female, except the companion of the woman sitting next to me. The sight of the women who were praying for me made me think a lot about how sympathetic women could be. It reminded me of an occasion when my mother was almost attacked by a mob in the ferry terminal for merely begging them to stop beating a suspected thief. I remember when someone in the crowd asked my mother why she risked her life by trying to beg for the suspected thief; her response was that every mother should. Now, seeing these women in the van, visibly concerned for my life, made me realize the importance of my mother's words.

6

As soon as the vehicle reached Banjul, I asked the driver for me to get off. Everyone watched in silence as I jumped from the van even before it came to a complete halt, with my bag dangling by my side. I immediately picked a taxi and asked the driver to rush to the ferry terminal.

I had missed the ferry. It was already on the north bank town of Barra, where I was headed. Since it had one more voyage to do for the night, I had to wait. There was heavy military presence around the gates of the ferry terminal. I stretched my arm through the side window of the room where tickets are sold and I bought one. Then I dashed out of the place instead of entering the waiting room. I went to the front beach adjacent to the ferry terminal and sat on the sand, the waves hitting hard and sometimes coming so close to me that I had to wriggle back a little. It was a lonely and secluded place. It was therefore a good place to keep myself somewhat invisible, but then again it also was dangerous for me because the tyrant's ubiquitous security operatives could whisk me away without the public noticing, which meant I could disappear forever.

While waiting for the ferry, I thought back to 2004 when I was appointed news editor of the Daily Observer, at the tender age of 24. That made me one of the youngest persons, if not the youngest, in the country to have ever occupied such a position. I felt challenged and exerted myself to prove I deserved the position.

Shortly after I assumed my editorial duties, I was given a special assignment to cover a commission of inquiry that investigated corruption among government officials. The commission was controversial, and many Gambians were upset with it because the president, who had set it up, did not present himself before it for scrutiny. Thus, many people derided the exercise as a sham.

When the commission initially started, two senior reporters covered its proceedings for the Daily Observer. However, a few days after they began covering it, officials of the Commission of Inquiry and some persons who had appeared before the Commission claimed that the two reporters had misquoted their testimonies. In fact, some of them threatened legal action against the paper if the reports in question were not retracted immediately and apologies made. As a result, the managing director himself wrote an apology and retracted the stories in question. Having placated the aggrieved persons, he took both reporters off the Commission beat and assigned me the task.

It was a big challenge, but given the fact that I had reported extensively on judicial stories for some time, I took the challenge in my stride and covered the remainder of the Commission's proceedings without any misrepresentation and my coverage increased the readership of the paper, both the physical and online editions.

However, my reporting did not go down well with some corrupt officials who had appeared before the Commission. Some of them were current and past ministers, including the vice president. Some of them were so corrupt that they could not explain to the Commission how they acquired their wealth. My reporting captured every detail of the humiliating episodes thus prompting some officials to threaten me with death. On some occasions, some would try to bribe me with money in an attempt to stop me from reporting their humiliating encounters at the commission. I rejected such offers, and I would inform some of my colleagues so that they would be my witnesses for possible future references. When those officials failed to bribe me, they resorted to all sorts of threats and harassment.

I know my kind of journalism had angered many people, especially those in authority. One day, when the commission sessions had ended for the week, I traveled to Sam-Mbollet to unwind. I had missed my mother so much and thus, wanted to spend some time with her – away from the bustle of the city. On my way to the village, I ran into my father who was returning from a district for a major by-election in the country. My father was an active member of the main opposition United Democratic Party (UDP). He was its chairperson in our native Lower Niumi constituency. He had no formal education but was good at speaking and mobilizing support for his political party. What led to that by-election was that the seat of the majority leader of the National Assembly who had fallen out with the president and subsequently got jailed was vacant and was being contested by the ruling party Alliance for Patriotic Re- orientation and Construction (APRC) and the UDP. My father had been away

43

from home, involved in that particular election until now. His party won a resounding victory.

The two of us boarded the ferry headed to the North Bank of the River Gambia. In the beginning, it was a joyful and beautiful voyage, as we enjoyed the gentle soothing tides of both the river and the Atlantic Ocean, and the breathtaking sight of leaping dolphins. My father radiated pure joy as he recounted to me how his party managed to snatch victory from the ruling party. He said because of the electoral defeat, the government had taken to harassing and arresting members of the opposition.

There was a man about the same age as my father, sitting near us. He knew my father and when they saw each other, they engaged in a long boring greeting. Baaba (father for Fula) introduced me to him. At some point, the two of them turned their conversation into politics, specifically the just ended by-elections. That man was a supporter of the ruling party and it was intriguing watching them discuss partisan politics. However, it was a mature and reasonable conversation regardless of their opposing political opinions. My father harped on the government's failed economic policies and poor human rights record as its bane.

All the while my father was chatting with his friend, there was a tall fellow standing in the opposite direction glowering at my father. I had seen him before. His name is Yero. He is the younger brother of the then interior minister. The tall fellow was a much-feared man in town, as many suspected him of being a member of the notorious NIA, the brutal secret state police.

All of a sudden, he interrupted my father and said, "You are a liar! You are the biggest liar I have ever seen. You are a stupid man! What you are saying is an insult to the president. Shut up!"

Yero's outburst took my father, his friend and everyone around by surprise. But not me. I sprang up, and, putting my head very close to his face, said, "You are the biggest liar; your father is the biggest liar in this world. In addition, you are the stupidest person in the world. Shut up!"

"You are insulting my father who is dead?" He said.

"Yes! You are stupid. You can do whatever you want in your power as a government agent. But I will not sit here and see you insult my father and be quiet," I said.

"Your father was insulting the president and you irresponsibly sat by, doing nothing to stop him. I will make sure your father is disciplined," he said and walked up the Ferry Captain area.

Before he disappeared, I told him that he could do whatever he wanted. "This country belongs to all of us. I will not be intimidated for doing nothing wrong. You can only kill me only once," I said.

He hesitated, grimaced at me and said, "You wait and see what will happen to you soon."

I did not care about the threat the thug had just made out against my father and me, but I was vigilant. I was watching every direction and carefully paying attention to every strange person around me.

While he was up the ferry captain area, I heard him talking on the phone. There were all indications that he was speaking with some people high up – probably his brother, the minister, or the president. I heard him saying that my father had insulted the president while "his son, an educated journalist who ought to know better, was sitting by and did not stop him. I want them to be taught a lesson".

Throughout that drama and afterwards, my father did not react or say a word to me. His friend and others around were also silent and looked confused about the incident. I was quiet too for the rest of the voyage, thinking about how my country had gone to the dogs. As the ferry anchored in Barra, and the hundreds of passengers were disembarking, police and plainclothes security personnel most of them armed to the teeth suddenly surrounded my father and me as we walked amongst the crowd. One of the plainclothes officers stretched out a pistol and said we were under arrest. By now, there were over a dozen security personnel encircling us. They warned us not to resist and urged us to follow them to the police station.

My father looked at me. He looked very sorry for me, and perhaps he felt guilty for putting me in trouble. By contrast, I felt bad with that kind of look and resisted it as much as I could, because as far as I was concerned, he was not responsible for any trouble. In fact, he was my hero. I looked at him without showing any sense of fear for what was going on. I was proud of him and I wanted him to see that in my face. So, let them do what they want. They are the ones who should be ashamed of themselves, I said to myself.

I smiled and made a sarcastic giggle that caught the attention of some of the armed security officers encircling us. One of my several peculiarities is that I mostly put my left hand in the pocket while walking. When one of the armed officers saw this, he exclaimed in the Wollof language, "Remove your hand from your pocket!"

I ignored him and walked on. He rushed on me, grabbed my hand and twisted it so hard out of my pocket that he almost broke my arm. He still held it. I stopped walking. Hundreds of people were watching.

"Leave my hand! Leave me alone!" I said.

My father said to me in Pulaar, our ethnic Fula language, "Don't say anything. Leave them."

I complied and kept quiet. Some sort of order returned, and we proceeded to the police station. When we got there, the station officer asked us to stand near the counter and give our statements. My father's friend, with whom he had been talking inside the ferry when the thug interrupted, followed us into the police station. He demanded that the security officers release us, telling them that we had done nothing wrong. No one paid him attention. Instead, the police kicked him out of the police station.

Yero also came to the police station and gave a statement laden with lies. As soon as he finished giving his statement, he turned to the station officer and ordered him to keep the two of us in the worst cell in the station.

Then he turned to me and said, "You think I don't know you? You are a journalist at the Daily Observer." "And so what?" I said.

The man was flippant and the more he talked, the better clues I had about what probably warranted his bullying. Is this about my work as a journalist? I thought it was about my father's position as an opposition member. Is it about my general reporting or my current reporting on the commission of inquiry and that the family of this thug could have been among the corrupt people who did not like my reporting? Whatever the reason, this man might have been stalking me. I do not care what warranted his actions against us, but someone has to stand up to tyranny.

"I will make sure you are fired from your job. You and your father don't like the president and his government," he said.

"Look…, do whatever you think you want to do, in the fastest manner you can. Otherwise, you can go to hell. I don't care!" I said.
The man charged at me and raised his hand to hit me. The station officer restrained him.

The station officer then addressed me: "I have heard that you are very rude. But I'm much ruder than you and I'll show it to you if you keep behaving rudely here."

Before I could respond, my father asked me to stop talking, and I complied, once again.

Then Yero said, "Lock them up. I will return here in two days and I want to see for myself that they have been punished."

I watched him as he jumped into his car that was parked outside the police station. I shook my head, looked at my father, our eyes met. Neither of us said anything. I squinted my eyes, looked the other way, and then gnashed my teeth.

The security officers left us standing for a long time without telling us anything. Some of the security officers were standing guard while some were crisscrossing the place, without saying a word. Finally, a group of security officers including the station officer came forward to the counter. The station officer said to the security officers in the Mandinka language: "Leave the little one to go and lock up the big one." Then he walked away into his office.

As soon as he finished talking, they grabbed my father, and pushed him into a caged hall where they temporarily detain people. I watched them pushing and maltreating my father. A certain officer yelled at me, "Get out of this place!"

I ignored him, and stood at the same spot, motionless.

When my father asked me to comply, I walked out and sat near a makeshift teashop across the road from the Barra Police Station. I sat musing for hours not knowing what to do. I called all my father's party members whom I could reach, and some of my friends and colleagues and family to inform them about what had happened. I bought an omelette sandwich with tea and took it to the police station so that my father would use it for dinner.

One officer screamed at me to leave the station or else they would lock me up as well. Just as the officer was ranting, a colleague of his took the sandwich from me but rejected the tin containing the tea. He told me a tin was not allowed in the police station because it was metal that cell inmates could use as a weapon to harm themselves or others. I thanked him and then went back to the teashop where I substituted the tin for a polythene bag and took it back to the police station.

From there, I sought out my aunt's husband who accompanied me to the police station. The police asked us out of the station and explained that my father could not see any visitors because he had been moved into one of the solitary confinement cells.

I was agonized and outraged. I could not imagine my father in a dark, filthy, mosquito-infested solitary cell in the torrid mid-summer weather. They were tiny cells and had just little openings for air at the top of the metal doors. I bent down near the roadside and wept my heart out, weighed down by a guilty feeling of having put my father in his present misery. I wiped my tears. Then my aunt's husband pulled me up in consolation. I was more worried about the terrible condition my father was currently encountering. I went to the shop again and bought a cold bottle of coca cola, poured it in a polythene bag and took it to the officers to give to him – hoping that it would cool him down. An officer gave it to him through a tiny opening on the metal door.

Then my aunt's husband and I went back to his home where I spent the night. The following morning, the two of us went to the police station in order to see my father. Most of my family and close relatives had gathered at the police station that morning as well. Much to our chagrin, the station officer informed us that he had been transferred across the river, to the capital city,

Banjul. I insisted that he told me where he was in Banjul and why he was taken there. He walked away and did not bother to respond.

That was one of the most dreadful moments in my life. The dictatorial government was fond of taking opponents to the torture bunkers at the much-feared National Intelligence Agency. I knew that it was possible that he would be tortured seriously or killed or go missing for good. His political party, the UDP, had informed me that their lawyer, Mariam Denton, would pursue the matter. But even if that would be useful, the lawyer wouldn't be able to do much until the weekend was over when the courts opened.

Therefore, it was worthless hanging around and beating a dead horse. Thus, my mother (who was among the family members who gathered at the police station that morning) and I went to our village, Sam-Mbollet.

First thing in the morning, that Monday, my mother, I, and other relatives went to the capital, Banjul, to seek out my father. We spent the whole day in Banjul. Despite the efforts of the lawyer and the opposition party, all the government officials and security officials that were confronted denied knowledge about his detention or his whereabouts. Politicians from other opposition parties also called me and offered that they would also pursue their own efforts to ensure that my father regained his freedom.

It took more than two weeks and my father was still detained incommunicado. When he was released – and as correctly expected, from the NIA bunkers – he was frail and weak. He told me that he had been repeatedly tortured and harassed during that period. According to him, several top government officials came to his detention place on a regular basis to coerce him to defect to the ruling party. He said they never talked to him about the reason for his arrest or about any charges that might be leveled against him. He said his refusal to accept their demands was the reason for his continuous detention and torture. And when they finally knew that he was not going to give in, they let him go. He saw himself as really lucky because if he were arrested in an isolated place, without the knowledge of other people, then he could have gone missing for good.

Shortly after my father's release, a shareholder of the observer company went personally to meet my managing director to demand that I be sacked. He is a businessman and a close ally of the dictator, Yahya Jammeh [who was being rumored to be, in fact, the secret owner of the Daily Observer.] But my managing director refused to give in to the government demands as he saw me as one of his best journalists and saw such an action as unjust. He said he would rather go with me than let me go.

It was getting late and dark, and the ferry was not yet in sight. It would be the last trip for the night. If I missed it, I would be in Banjul, until the next day. The thought of spending the night in Banjul made me shiver in fear and desperation.

There were a few restaurants still open. I went inside one of them and ordered a chicken sandwich while I sat at a corner table. It was secluded, so I considered myself safe. I had only one bite of the chicken sandwich. As soon as I swallowed it, I threw up. My vomit messed up the tablecloth and the floor. I tried to stand up, but I could not as I felt a sharp pain rip through my stomach. A waiter rushed to me to support me. When she saw the state I was, she dashed back to the counter and brought me a bottle of Coca Cola and asked me to drink it. I took a few gulps, left some money on the table and sneaked out of the restaurant. I had to do everything to be as anonymous as possible – and I did not know who was inside the restaurant, and what they knew.

Out of the restaurant, I slunk around the terminal vicinity, avoiding places where I could easily be recognized. I was at a loss as to what to do. My phone rang incessantly, but I ignored it. Now and again, I felt like throwing up, and whenever the urge came, I would bend down and spit out a sour-tasting thick substance.

By now the ferry was about to anchor in Banjul. With my head aching persistently, I decided to listen to some music to ease the pain. When I put on my headphone, I saw that it was acting up and I had to buy new ones. I scanned the surroundings to make sure that there was no suspicious figure lurking in the gathering darkness. Satisfied that there was no immediate danger, I swept into a Guinean-Fula shop and grabbed one set of headphones.

Just then, I saw a lanky fellow leaning towards me. My heart skipped a beat, fearing that I had walked right into the arms of a secret security agent, because Banjul is awash with them. As I was trying to twist myself away from him, he leaned even closer to me and whispered in a Senegalese Wollof accent: "Don't buy that headphone. It is not good. It will get damaged within a few days."

Then I regained my composure.

The ferry had now fully anchored and vehicles and passengers were disembarking. In a matter of few minutes, I would be joining it in order to get to the other side of the country and then escape into neighbouring Senegal. When it was time for the ferry to take on board new passengers, I went to a gate where scores of passengers were scrambling to get on the ferry. All around were soldiers, lashing out at the crowd with whips. Two soldiers in particular were watching to see who was joining the crowd. I was scared because I did not want the soldiers to see me; worse still, I was worried that if I missed the ferry, I could be in greater danger. I then retreated to a nearby shop run by a Mauritanian to keep an eye on both soldiers. Luckily, I saw them move a few paces away from the gate and lit their cigarettes. Taking my chance, I tore into the crowd, squeezed myself through a fence and joined the throng milling around the ferry. I climbed to the highest deck of the ferry and sat in a quiet corner.

A few minutes after the ferry began tearing through the water, a call came in again. It was Sheriff Bojang Junior yet again. He reiterated his admonition for me to get out of the country quickly and said he would try all he could to see if he could get somebody to lodge me when I reached Senegal. I told him that I was somewhere on my way out of the country. I did not mention the place I was because I was afraid that someone somewhere could be eavesdropping on my phone conversations. Sheriff kept calling to check on me throughout the rest of the journey.

Another person from my newspaper called. I was curious why he was calling me because he was not only notorious for his blind and open support for the dictatorship, but he also bragged about his so-called closeness to the powers that-be.

"Hello," I said.

"Hello, Omar! Omar Bah! Is this Omar?" He screamed over the phone.

"Yes. It's me."

"But, Omar where are you? What I am hearing..., is it true? I heard that the soldiers are all over town looking for you."

I managed to force out a giggle. "I've heard about it. It is not true. Actually, it is another Omar Bah. Do not worry, okay. I am on my bed listening to Fula music. I'll talk to you later."

"But this is very serious you know. I just want to make sure that you are safe. You know I support this government, so if I am worried like this, then you should know that it is very serious. Whatever the case is, make sure you are careful, okay. Bye."

The ferry anchored at Barra. As I walked among the crowd toward the gates in order to get out of the terminal, I saw many security personnel keeping sentries at the gates. Some were standing by the fences, while some were holding some communication devices and guns, crisscrossing the area. I kept moving, hoping that I could still melt into the crowd and remain invisible. However, the further I went, the tighter the security became. There was no way I could get out of the terminal. Now, I was trapped. My only exit from the river was now impossible. I backed off quickly, running in between the disembarking passengers back to the ferry. As I ran back into the ferry, someone shouted, "Hey!"

I pretended that I did not hear the call. I ran even faster. When I glanced back, I noticed it was someone in the overall uniform of the ferry workers. He was hot on my heels, probably thinking I was some cheat trying to get into the ferry without a ticket. When I got inside, I hid under the wooden benches inside one of the ferry cabins. He ran fast past where I was hiding, flashing his torch-light everywhere. The place was dark and empty. Even though my pursuer was a ferry worker, I did not want to create any scene that could attract the atten-tion of the police or the soldiers, which would be like giving meat to a hungry hyena.

After some time, when passengers started getting on board the ferry to cross over back to Banjul, I got out. Then I walked for about one hundred meters toward the gates and stood at one spot in the middle of the crowd, whilst I peered around. I did not see any security personnel. Security might have re-laxed because they might have thought that everyone had disembarked and now that the ferry was loading to return to the other side of the river, they might have seen it a waste of time and energy to stay at the arrival gates. Therefore, I took a gamble – I walked through the gates, running and stopping now and then to look over my shoulders to see whether one of the soldiers might still be lurking in the dark.

As soon as the terminal gates were behind me, I began running at full speed. My bag handle that was dangling over my shoulder cut off and the bag fell. I turned around to pick up the bag, and then scampered away. I took the dusty road leading into Barra. I had to be extra careful because the road was adjacent the Barra Police Station. Even though there were no police officers hanging outside the station, I could not take chances as I did not know what to expect. On the other edge of the road, there were a lot of shanty stalls and dilapidated walls. I placed myself on that side of the road until I was a distance away from the police station. I was heading to a relative's house.

At the last intersection before taking a turn to get to my relative's house, my cell phone rang.

"Hello. Omar Bah." It was a woman.

"Yes, who is this?" The woman identified herself. She was an acquaintance.

She asked me where I was and kept repeating the question. Her tone sounded as if she was under some sort of duress to locate my whereabouts. At that mo-ment, I did not want to give trust a chance. Therefore, just as I did with the government supporter who had called me earlier, I gave her the same response. After her call, I did not know whom to trust as a friend or who was a traitor. From that point on, I switched off my cell phone and walked into my relative's compound.

There were some people sitting and lying on mats and bamboo beds in the courtyard, brewing green tea. I went straight into the house and sat on the arm of the chair near the door without greeting anyone. When my cousins saw me, they jumped up and hugged me. I asked the older girl to go call their mother who was outside and apparently did not see me when I entered the compound. The girl soon rushed back into the room, and stood near me, happy that I had visited.

I asked her to give me some water to drink, while I fixed the handle of my bag that had cut off earlier. As I was drinking the water, their mother burst into the room, looking nervous and scared. She suspected that I was in deep trouble, as she already knew about the problem with the media.

"Omar, is it peace?" She said.

"No. It is not peace. The government is looking for me. There are heavily armed soldiers all around town and my workplace looking for me. If they catch me, they will kill me."

As soon as I said that, she placed both of her hands on her head and sobbed uncontrollably. She knelt down, stood up, ran out of the room, and stood at the veranda, weeping. Her husband who was sitting on a bamboo bed in the middle of the compound courtyard ran in to console her and asked what had happened. She told him. As people around the compound began to gather, she turned to me and said, "What are you going to do now, my child? God, help me!"

She went on crying and praying.

I rose, grabbed my bag and headed toward the door. I was afraid I had caused too much attention already. She pulled me back.

"Where are you going?" She asked. Then she asked her older daughter to bring me more water again. I took the cup of water and gulped it down. Her husband came into the room and asked me what I was going to do. When I told him that I wanted to flee the country, he told me to do so immediately before his wife's cries would draw more attention. Then I grabbed my bag and rose. The woman grabbed me yet again. When I stopped and looked at her, she said, "So where are you going to stay? Where are you going?"

"I will go to Senegal. I don't know where in Senegal I'm heading to yet, but I will sort that out if I make it."

"What will you eat, my child?"

"I've some money with me. I can have enough transport fare and food with it until I reach."

I walked away.

She grabbed me and pulled me back again. "Wait!" She said.

Her husband intervened and asked her to leave me to go if she wanted me alive. "Close your eyes, lift your right leg and pray," she said. "Then step outside the door with that same right leg."

As soon as I did that, I rushed out of the compound. I could hear her crying, and people consoling her as I vanished into the dusty streets.

7

I avoided taking one straight street. I knew that town well, because I lived there during the latter part of my senior secondary school education. I kept taking tiny streets and cutting into others—through dark corners—until I got to the car park. There were no commercial vehicles heading for the border village of Amdalaye, except for a few taxis packed around. I approached a young man leaning on his taxi, for hire. I was not sure how much I had on me but I estimated I could reach my destination, Dakar, the capital of Senegal, even if the taxi driver overcharged me.

"Amdalaye? In this late night? Well, brother you have to pay two hundred dalasis."

I knew he had quadrupled the price, but I was in no condition to haggle prices. All I wanted was to get a car to take me across the border into the safety of Senegal. "Okay, let's go. I've no time."

He grabbed his shirt from the top of the roof of his car and motioned me inside the taxi. He drove a few meters and branched to a gas station. As we left, I asked him, "Won't you wear your shirt?"

"No brother. It's so hot!"

I wondered where the heat was coming from. Despite all the running I had done that night, I was now feeling chills in my body. When he revved the engine, I turned to him and asked him to drive at a speed because I had no time to waste.

He kept driving. Whatever speed he ran was never enough for me. He understood what was in my looks very well because the more I tilted my head toward him and stared, the faster he drove. Suddenly, just after the major health

53

center at Essau, by the big baobab tree at the intersection, torchlight flashed up and down in the middle of the road.

Oh God, that must be a security checkpoint. I am dead. I was so scared that I had to hold and pull the hand of the driver, willing him to stop so that I could jump out and vanish into the town. However, before I could say anything, he had wriggled his hand out of my grip and stopped at the checkpoint. Two police officers were standing in the middle of the road by a road sign with the inscription: 'STOP. POLICE'

One of them walked to the door of the driver and asked him to show the papers of his car. While the police officer was talking to the driver, my hand was on the door handle ready to open it and jump out if it need be. After skimming through the driver's papers, the police officer bent and peered at me from the window of the driver's door. There was no light inside the old rickety car, and since the officer did not point his light at me, he could not really see my face. However, I was not willing to surrender at that point, and so I held on to the door handle firmly. I was nervous but managed to maintain focus. I kept looking ahead in order to avoid the officer seeing my face. After some time, he asked in the Mandinka language, "Who is it?"

"It's me," I said in a low sluggish tone in the same language. Still, I refused to tilt my head toward him.

Though he did not ask any more questions, he kept looking at me for a little while. Then he nodded and made a sound: "huuu." He stood straight and ordered the driver to open the trunk of the car. After a brief inspection, he let us go. As soon as the car started moving, I breathed and felt safe.

The driver revved the engine once again. As we were getting near the outskirts of Essau, I saw the compound where my maternal grandmother used to live when she was alive, and I remembered how many times I had stayed there with my mother and siblings. It was heart wrenching to think that I might never see that compound in my life again.

Soon, we drove past several villages in the locality where I grew up. Midway into the journey, we were near Sam-Mbollet, my home village. The closer we were to my village, the sadder I became. I could not face the reality that I might be seeing these places for the last time in my life – if there would be any such life for me. At exactly about ten kilometers into the journey, we reached Njongon, which is at about halfway to the border. When we approached the St. Michael's School by the gmelina and neem groves in the centre of the linear village, I asked the driver to stop. A new wave of emotions and nostalgia engulfed me again. I spent my childhood school years at St. Michael's, the great memories of which were hard to pass by. Opposite the school, right across the road we were driving on, was the dirt road leading to my village,

Sam-Mbollet. It stretched out just about three kilometers into the bush. Tilting my head toward that road, I realized that I had to do something quickly before leaving the country. *My mother! I must see my mother for the last time.* "Please take that road and take me to Sam-Mbollet. It is my village. I just have to pass by before proceeding," I said to the driver. He did not seem to like it. In fact, he told me that he was not going to do it.

"No. I cannot risk driving through that dusty and bumpy road. It will finish off my gas. You should have informed me earlier so that I would buy more gas. I cannot go there," he said.

I sighed and stared at the dirt road leading to my village.

Everyone in Njongon village seemed asleep, and thus it was completely silent. Other than the sounds of crickets, and occasional dogs' barks, there was no other sign of life. The driver revved the engine and burst into a sudden speed once again.

"So you are from Sam-Mbollet?" The driver asked, as he sped on. "Yes,"

He started mentioning names of his friends and relatives in my village. Coincidentally, some of the people he mentioned were my relatives as well. He told me the name of his village where I also have some relatives. The truth is that we were distant relatives in one way or the other. However, I did not care to know. He seemed to have also suspected that we were related because, even though I did not tell him my name or my ethnic group, he stopped speaking Wollof to me and started speaking in my Fula language, Pulaar. He however seemed jittery that I was taciturn. Since the car was dark inside, we could not make out each other's face, which was just as well in that if he were to be arrested later on and quizzed about who his 'mystery' passenger was, he probably could not give them information about what I looked like.

The driver kept talking and throughout his monologue, I kept quiet and occasionally nodded. He drove until we could sight some flashes of lights at the border village of Amdalaye in the distance. Then I asked him to stop the car – in the middle of nowhere. He made such an abrupt stop that both of us bumped to the front of the vehicle. He stared at me for a while without saying anything.

"What is it, brother?" He asked. "Why are we stopping at this place?"

I ignored him. I just counted his money, paid him, and hopped out of the car. As I started walking away, into the open fields of bushes and shrubs where hyenas were howling, the driver came out pleading with me to get back into the car. He said he could take me up to my destination, as it was not safe to be in the middle of the bush at that time of the night with the hyenas.

I neither responded nor turned back. At some point, the driver gave up, got into his car, and drove away. It was dark and scary as hyenas were all around the area. I walked through the bushes and through the outskirts of the village, carefully avoiding being spotted, and avoiding any sign of a human being. I kept walking, sometimes almost tiptoeing and lowering my body, until I got into the first Senegalese border town of Karang. When I got inside the town, I kept walking as deep inside as possible until the difference of the architecture of the houses proved that I was indeed inside Senegal. However, I had to make sure – I asked somebody who walked past me in a narrow street, who confirmed to me that I was inside Senegal.

I sat in a quiet corner at a tiny side street to reflect on my life as a journalist. It was hard to imagine that I was now outside my country and never to return again, and probably never to see my wife and family again – and probably never to practice my profession again. As I sat at the quiet corner, with my back against a straw fence, and my face in between my knees, I tried to make sense of my fate.

I had been a journalist for nearly six years now. It had been an exciting but demanding journey. When I looked back, it seemed to me that the journey had been going on forever. It all began in late 1999, when I had to go to the city to fend for myself after completing my high school education. It was a cool autumn night in the village when my father bade me farewell.

"Alhaji", my father had said, as he turned back to the prayer congregation. He was referring to his friend, Alhaji Mam Pateh. "I want us to pray for Omar."

With that, they showered prayers and praises and advice on me far into the night. The Ramadan month of fasting had just ended. I had lived in the compound for the past months since I completed my senior secondary education, leading the rest of the children in the compound's subsistence farm work.

"This son of mine," my father said.

Everyone in the compound was still sitting down in his or her prayer lanes. I had led the prayers that night, and was now sitting, cross-legged and facing the rest of the congregation.

"I qualify him today of being capable of even looking after my family should I die, today. I see everything in him that I want in a son."

I pressed my heart repeatedly. I wanted to cry, but I was able to suppress the tears. I just kept looking down, listening to the speeches, and slowly hitting my forehead with my right palm and saying "Amen" in an apparent acceptance of the prayer.

After my father had finished his monologue, it was his friend's turn to speak. He thanked my father for being so generous to me. Just like the way he was a friend to my father, he had also been a very good friend of mine. He knew I wanted to speak and say "thank you" to my father and everybody and seek for continuous prayer and blessing as I set out to face the real world outside my family. Because I was tense, he did it on my behalf. He thanked my father on my behalf and informed him that I had always been very appreciative of everything my father had been doing for me, and that I wanted prayers wherever I went. It took long before we dispersed that night. At the end, I was in a paradoxical state of being – very emotional, but very elated and encouraged.

Towards the end of the year 1999, when the whole work in the compound and farms was ready, I packed a few things in a traveling bag and set out to go to the city. In the days before I left, my father had been trying to convince me to become a teacher. He would argue that most of those who completed senior secondary education had already been absorbed into the schools as unqualified teachers. He would say that I ought to give that a thought as it was a ready guarantee for a job, so that I could help the family. Whenever he brought up that topic, I would just smile, giggle, and say nothing. I did not hate teaching, but there were things I would like to prioritize first. When he finally realized that I did not want to be pressured or given excessive opinions about what I wanted to do, he left me alone and just resorted to praying for me and encouraging me.

I was filled with emotions again the day I left the village. I saw it as 'my second leaving', the first being my sojourn to the city for high school education. Nevertheless, I was happy that this time around, I was no longer a child or a student, and would rather scavenge than go hungry or be maltreated by others merely for accommodating me. I was a twenty-year old stepping into the real world.

I had not had a place to stay in the city yet. My mother had done everything possible to mend fences between one of her younger sisters in the city and me – I had had trouble with her during the initial part of my high school years. Though the strain had worn off, I was still not comfortable going to live there full-time. I decided to go to Barra, the last town before crossing the river and to the city. My mother had another younger sister there with whom I stayed with during the latter part of my high school years. I was more comfortable living with her, though it would have been more convenient for me to live with the one in the city. For a start, I could stay in Barra so that I would occasionally take the ferry voyage and go to the city and look for a job or some further educational opportunities.

After some thought, I decided that I was not going to look for a job. I enrolled at the Gambia Technical Training Institute for a two-year national diploma in law. If I were able to complete that program, it was going to be a stepping-stone to becoming a lawyer someday. It was not going to be easy, because the two-year program was the highest law course available in my country. I had to go to another West African country in order to get a degree in law. However, I was determined—one step at a time.

When I got admission into the institute, I told my father about it. He was furious that I had defied his wish of getting a job. Besides, many people in my society believe that lawyers are liars and hypocrites and thus hell bound. Even though the leader of my father's main opposition party was a lawyer, I knew it would still be hard to convince him that being a lawyer was okay. He vowed that he was not going to pay anything towards that educational program. I started going to school, nonetheless.

The classes were held in the evening shift and that made my traveling across the river easier. Sometimes when the classes were late and I missed the ferry, I would spend the night at my aunt's home in the city.

A few days after I started classes, I was kicked out of school for not paying school fees. I talked to my father over and over, but he would not budge. One day, after being away from classes for a while, I caught up in town with Mr Omigie, the coordinator of the Law Programme. He was elated to see me, as according to him, he was starting to get worried about my absence. When I explained to him my problem, he asked me to invite my father to his office for a meeting; he promised to talk to him on my behalf.

Teachers are highly respected people in Gambian society, so it was not too difficult to convince my father to agree to meet Mr Omigie. As both of us were going together for him to meet Mr Omigie, he made it clear to me that he was just going out of respect for the teacher but would not be convinced into paying any fees for my school. We arrived early before class. There was only one student, one Ousman Camara. Mr Omigie welcomed us into his office. Because he was a Nigerian by origin, he was not fluent in the widely spoken Wollof language. Likewise, my father could not speak English, and I was not a suitable candidate for interpreting. Mr Omigie therefore called the student, Ousman, to interpret during the meeting.

After a long discussion, Mr Omigie was able to convince my father that I should be encouraged to do the course. He told my father that my senior secondary school results were very good and that the biggest mistake my father would make was not to encourage me to go ahead with my studies. He went on and on trying to convince my father, and by the end of the meeting, my father gave his word that he was going to sponsor me. I was elated. As I walked my father down the stairs, he smiled and said, "Omar. He does whatever he says."

My father paid part of the school fees. It was tough for him despite the efforts he was making. The Law program of the institute had a link with some educational institutions in London, the UK. At some point, during our first year, we wrote an exam that was graded in London. When the results came back, I was first in the class, followed by one Abdul Jobe. When I told my father, he was ecstatic and promised to continue to support me in my academic pursuits. However, I was lucky that Mr Omigie found me some scholarship to complete the course.

The competition in my class was stiff. I would spend long hours at the Law section of the school library reading. Because I would spend a long time in the library, I developed a habit of reading newspapers every day. I would make sure I read the articles and editorials of the *Daily Observer, The Point* and *The Independent* newspapers. They were the main newspapers in the country. I eventually became so attached to the papers that I memorized most of their bylines. When I was in senior secondary school, I used to read newspapers, but not as habitually as now. I had always had a great interest in politics. In my high school days, I would go to parliament to watch parliamentary debates, and to seize the opportunity to see the politicians in person. I would also go to the courts to see lawyers in their gowns and wooly wigs – a sight I found scary in the beginning. Now that I was a law student bound to wear that wig and gown someday, I visited the courts more often. Our lecturers always advised us to make time to attend court sittings in order to have a pragmatic experience of the operations of the legal system. It was in the courts and in the parliamentary sittings that I began to learn more and know much more about the practice of law and the governance system in the country. I knew outright that the kind of government we had in place was utterly dictatorial, with the kinds of policies they had in place through parliamentary bills easily passed through a rubber-stamp parliament of which a commanding majority belonged to the ruling party; and the kinds of trumped up charges they used to proffer against political opponents.

My enrollment as a law student was what catapulted me into the real world of politics. The more I understood what was going on in my country, the more I understood why it was necessary for people to speak up against tyranny. By now, it was more than apparent that what we had in place was a dictatorship, with the president as an absolute authority in the country.

When the president took overpower in a military coup some years earlier, he came in as a very poor person who personally confessed to his poverty and hence identified with the poor people in the country. His apparent vitamin deficiency vividly showed in the sores on the sides of his lips when he newly took overpower. Most people were hopeful that, given his background, he was going to love the country and, in fact, hand over power immediately to a civilian government.

Before our very eyes, Yahya Jammeh metamorphosed into a firespitting dragon. He removed the section of the constitution that stipulated presidential term limits, banned some political parties, built a city out of his home village, owned commercial farms and businesses, and started driving in fleets of luxury cars. He said he would be in power for as long as he wanted, a direct contradiction to the reason he claimed for overthrowing his predecessor.

Apart from stealing the country blind, President Yahya Jammeh had shown utter contempt for Gambians. He had also killed so many people that it is hard to keep count of his victims. He even had the guts to address the people on national television and brag about the fact that he was now a very rich man. He said his money came from "Allah's World Bank". He also told the nation that he had become so rich that even his great-great grandchildren would never smell the scent of poverty. His clownish attitude was worrying and embarrassing to Gambians, when he would dress in abnormally large kaftans, turbans, three pairs of prayer beads, a sword, and a copy of the Holy Quran, with a barrage of bogus titles added to his name – *Sheikh, Professor, Doctor, Alhaji…...* Jammeh is a one-man circus show. However, that was nothing compared to his dictatorial and childish demeanour and utterances. I could not just believe that a character like Yahya Jammeh was what was ruling the greatly peaceful and hospitable country of The Gambia – an absolute dictator.

The economy had collapsed to a level that the dalasi (the country's currency) had lost its value three-fold against the dollar. Cost of living had become so high that most families eliminated the traditional three-square meal a day. Most would have only the shared afternoon lunch. Doors of mosques and churches, and major junctions were continuously crowded with unusual large crowds of beggars, accosting worshippers, pedestrians and motorists. The tourism industry was collapsing because of the number of jobless and hungry people begging visitors on the beaches and hotel areas. Even though tourists liked the country for its beauty, some felt exceedingly harassed by the streams of beggars pestering them wherever they went.

Agriculture was in shambles. The country's main cash crop, ground- nut, was rendered meaningless as there was no significant market for it, and no meaningful industry through which farmers could earn income; or revenue accrual for the country. Corruption was a lucrative industry for thieves masquerading as government employees. The Customs and Excise, Police, Ports Authority and almost all sectors of the nation have become so corrupt that most of the revenue they were collecting ended up in their private pockets. The rate of car accident deaths was competing, if not superseding the number of deaths caused by diseases. The worse thing about it was the fact that most of the deaths caused by car accidents could have been averted if the police were not corrupt. Most police officers on the traffic would let traffic offenders go as long as they could pass a few notes of money to them. In most cases, people obtained driver's licenses without being qualified as long as they were ready to part with money. Vehicles without proper brakes were on the rampage in town causing an untold number of deaths. Junior Customs and Excise staff lived in the kind of luxury that even tycoons could barely afford. Moreover, the worst of the national calamities was the huge life of luxury and extravagance President Yahya Jammeh himself and his cronies lead, in total disregard to the poverty-stricken people of The Gambia. Brutality through arbitrary arrests, torture and detention without trial and refusal to comply with court orders, and murder with impunity, were the order of the day. The only thing the government could deliver was that act of brutality in utter negligence of their responsibility of service to the people. The prices of gas had been increasing almost every month, and when drivers increased their transport fares in line with the increase of gas prices, the government would arrest and torture them. The government would not admit that life was like hell in The Gambia. I could not imagine how some people in power could be so selfish – because life was fine with them through their illicit fortune; they would not admit that life was tough and unbearable for the rest of the people.

But all these were only to be whispered in private, as a culture of secret spying and fear had already been instilled in the people, with the use of the highly lethal political police, the National Intelligence Agency, the July 22nd Movement; and the Green Boys. Since Jammeh came to power, countless coup scares had been announced by the dictator which would eventually be used as a pretext to kill and/or mass-bury perceived opponents; and for detentions incommunicado; sackings from jobs; and torture.

One day, after the announcement of one of such monotonous attempted coups in the country in the year 2000, some soldiers were killed. Many others were rounded up and tortured and detained incommunicado. In reaction to the so-called coup attempt, President Yahya Jammeh appeared on national television to address the nation and said: "More heads will roll, and I'll swim in blood!" Yet on another occasion, the president, while threatening his oppo nents, said he would not hesitate to "kill twenty thousand Gambians" in order to "save" the remaining people in the country, if he realized that the opposition wanted to destabilize the country. With all those happenings in my country, I had concluded that I was going to do something with my life that would make me fight for the oppressed and speak for the voiceless in my society. In the year 2000, a paramilitary officer attacked a thirteen-year old student at a beach party and raped her. In addition to that, another student, Ebrima Barry, died after seven state security officers allegedly arrested and tortured him. By then, the Gambia Students' Union (Gamsu) had become impatient and frustrated at the seeming impunity the dictatorship had inculcated in security officers in the country. Therefore, the leadership of Gamsu under its president, Omar Joof, wrote several protest letters to the authorities demanding that the two gravely serious cases be prosecuted immediately. Despite several minor street marches and requests and lobbying, the authorities remained defiant and behaved as if nothing had happened. Finally, on 10 April 2000, the students in the country decided to embark on a peaceful march in the streets in order to show indignation at what had happened to their colleagues. As soon as the students gathered to begin their march, the regime deployed heavily armed military and other security personnel to stop the march. I was at the center of it all. I remember when I arrived at West Field Junction, the biggest intersection in the city of Serrekunda, soldiers were all over the place beating and arresting students. I joined the leadership of Gamsu trying to organize the students in order to avoid a confrontation with the security forces who were only interested in attacking the students. Our efforts bore naught. I remember how the president of Gamsu wearing a very rough hair that morning, crisscrossed the streets appealing for calm. The situation was already out of control as there were thousands of security forces and students with each group charging at each other. At some point, I saw some students lying in pools of blood, severely wounded. Initially, the soldiers used rubber bullets only, but later, they started using life rounds. I was among a group of students standing by a fence on a side street when all of a sudden, a mass of students ran helter skelter past us, warning that the security was now firing live bullets, and that several people had already been killed. Before they finished, more gunshots were heard nearby. We all ducked behind a cement fence. Now, it was a matter of how to get home unscathed. I had the advantage of not being easily identifiable because I was not wearing a uniform being a tertiary student, unlike the normal school children. Nevertheless, the soldiers did not care about that, and so I had to be extremely careful as the soldiers were shooting randomly. When I finally got home, I heard over the radio an announcement that one of those killed was one Omar Barrow, a popular radio journalist and Red Cross volunteer.

On 11 April 2000, the day after the student demonstration in the city, the students in the provinces also took to the streets in solidarity with their colleagues. Again, heavily armed state security officers prevailed upon them and shot many of them dead. Apart from the dead, several more students who sustained gunshot injuries were maimed for life.

After the disturbances, a coroner's inquest and later a commission of inquiry looked into the matter of the incident to find out those responsible for the killings. The regime eventually closed all the schools in the country indefinitely.

Because of the closure of the schools, I returned to the village. By the time I came back to the city after the schools were re-opened by the regime, the coroner's inquest had ended and the commission of inquiry begun. I made it a point of duty to attend the proceedings of the commission regularly. Members of the public were allowed to ask witnesses questions. I would always ask questions, which were copiously reported in the media. Eventually, I became acquaintance with most of the journalists who were covering the proceedings. At the end of its findings, the Commission of Inquiry identified the state security agents who killed the students. The Commission's findings contradicted Vice President Isatou Njie-Saidy's initial lies to the nation that the students themselves had shot one another. Unsurprisingly, the government reacted to the commission's report by rushing to its rubber stamp national assembly to enact a law that indemnified all the security officers who were named in the report. That was the end of the case. Consequently, the culprits continued to walk as free people with impunity after gunning down at least fourteen helpless children, including a journalist.

This was the socio-political milieu I found myself in after my high school education. I thought I needed to do something that would enable me to express my awakening – and help speak for the voiceless and ultimately to stand up against tyranny. I had been contemplating writing for some time now especially since after the student demonstrations. Through my interactions with journalists during the Commission's sittings and various court sittings, the profession fascinated me so much, so that I decided to take a leap in the dark. One fine morning in August 2000, on my way to school, I decided to pass through the offices of the bi-weekly *The Independent* newspaper. I had been contemplating training as a reporter for a while, and had now decided to talk to some editors to see whether

I would be given the opportunity.

When I climbed up the steps of the newspaper offices, I found some people in the first room I entered and then asked for the editor. They pointed to an office adjacent where they were sitting and motioned me to walk in. I knocked on the door to the editor's office and someone peering above huge scholastic goggles and leafing through piles of papers on his desk waved me in. It was my first time to see him but given the fact that his photo byline always accompanied his powerful weekly essays, it was easy to recognize that it was Baba Galleh Jallow, the editor-in-chief of *The Independent*. After shaking hands and sitting down, he asked me what he could do for me.

"Are you the editor?" I said. "Yes."

"Well...," I said. "My name is Omar Bah. I graduated from Gambia Senior Secondary School about a year ago. I am now a law student at GTTI. As a result, I am often at the courts and many other places of journalistic interest. On many occasions, I witness very important court cases but they go unreported because journalists are usually not there. I therefore want to begin training as a journalist by writing for you when I find something that might interest you. I think I will be able to do something from time to time on a part-time basis given the fact that I am a student."

Throughout the time I was talking, the editor occasionally peered at me from above his huge scholastic goggles that were resting on his nose. I had always been a huge fan of his wonderful writing and felt seriously intimidated sitting with him. However, I could see in his face that he was interested in what I had just said.

He told me that he would be happy if I could do that, adding that I could start with the courts. Before I left, he told me that *The Independent* was a small newspaper and thus, could not hire many people on a full-time basis. Nevertheless, he said, like many other reporters, I would be paid per published article. He also promised me that that if I worked hard, he would consider me for the occasional in-house training clinics that the newspaper conducted for rookie reporters. Before I left, he stressed that stories had to be accurate, and written in good English.

"Thank you, sir. Thank you," I said, as I bolted out of the door. A few days later, I got my first two stories published in prominent positions in the paper. One of the stories was about the taking of not guilty pleas of security officers accused of killing Student Ebrima Barry that had triggered the students' demonstrations. The other story was on the sorry state of the ferry terminals on the crossing points of the River Gambia. I could not stop drooling over my bylines in the paper, taking the paper with me wherever I went and staring at my bylines now and again. As my excitement mounted, I resolved to take writing seriously, giving it my all. I reported extensively from the courts – so much so that my colleagues nicknamed me 'Court' or 'Justice'.

8

I walked down some narrow dark streets until I reached the main road inside the Senegalese border town of Karang. I approached some currency dealers who converted the remainder of the Gambian currency into the CFA franc, the common currency of 14 francophone West and Central African countries, including Senegal.

Then I bounded to the car park to board a car to Dakar. There was only one seven-passenger car that was going to Dakar, and midnight was fast approaching. If I missed the car, it meant I would have to spend the night at Karang. I did not want that – the farther I was from The Gambia, the safer for me. The car was not full yet, so I asked the driver whether he could guarantee me a seat while I rushed to the mosque at the corner of the car park to pray. When he agreed, I placed my handbag on the middle seat of the back row and ran to the mosque. After finishing my prayers, I sat inside the mosque for a while, alone, thanking God more than ever. I did not even realize I was speaking aloud. The truth was that I could not believe that I had gotten out of The Gambia.

The driver left Karang at exactly midnight. As he drove on, I was alert and suspicious of two hefty people who sandwiched me, thinking of what to do if they should attempt anything against me. The silence in the car was even scarier. Just a few kilometers into the journey, our car broke down. The driver parked by the side of the road and opened the bonnet to examine something. I was scared, thinking it was a ploy to have the car stop in the middle of nowhere for me to be kidnapped and returned to The Gambia. Whenever a car was approaching from the direction of The Gambia while our car was still being fixed, I would bend down and turn to the opposite direction to avoid being

65

recognized. I was relieved when everyone got back inside the car and the driver sped away. Along the way, one of the passengers said he was getting off the car, but the driver said others were free to get off as well to take fresh air and stretch their legs for a few minutes. When I stepped down, someone pulled my shoulder from behind. I froze. In that instant I knew the Gambian authorities had gotten me at last and wondered why they would go to such lengths to have me arrested and killed. As I was about to surrender, I heard the person who had pulled my shoulder from behind say *Na nga def[1]* with a Senegalese accent. The voice was vaguely familiar, but I could not tell where I heard it before. Then I turned. I nearly fainted in relief. It was the Senegalese who had advised me against buying the headphones at the Banjul ferry terminal hours earlier. He bade farewell and disappeared into the night.

At about four in the morning on Tuesday, 30 May 2006, I arrived at the main car park in Dakar. The driver had really sped – the journey that had to take at least six hours was competed in less than five hours. When we got off the car, the passengers headed in different directions except me – I did not know where to go. It was still dark. With no sense of direction, I roamed the huge car park, with my blue handbag hanging over my shoulder, for an hour or so. Later when morning beckoned and it was beginning to get bright, I strode into some of the streets nearby which were already filled with beggars and traders. As I walked slowly past, I dropped some coins as charity in the palms of some beggars. Some of them would pray that God gave me protection as if they knew that 'protection' was what I needed most in my life at that point in time. At some point, I saw the Senegalese national television station and thought back to 2004 when I visited there with my journalism classmates. I wondered when I would see all those friends and when I would have the freedom to interact with all of them back home once again. If someone had told me that I would one day return to Dakar wandering its streets as a fugitive, I would have spat on his or her face.

I walked a few blocks further down the street. The sun had risen now and the streets were full of people. I walked past a mini stadium Along the way, one of the passengers said he was getting off the streets, and a highly congested street market. As I kept roaming around the streets, I realized that the zip of my pants had been damaged. I could not remember when it had happened. I pulled out the front of my shirt and held it down to cover the exposure until I got a tailor to mend the zip.

The time on my cell phone showed that it was already nine in the morning. I had to look for a cybercafé. Perhaps there was information or important emails from friends and colleagues that I should see. As soon as I found one, I paid for a thirty-minute usage. Inside the cybercafé, there were some telephone booths. I decided to make some calls first before checking my emails. It was important to call some phone numbers. I had to see whether someone could host me. I had two telephone numbers for one Pa Louis Thomasi. He was a Gambian who lived and worked in Senegal. I had attended the same conference with him in the Ivory Coast a month earlier. However, I could not get him on both lines, so I decided to check my mails now because Sheriff, who had advised me to escape the night before, had mentioned to me that he would contact some people in Senegal to help me. Probably he had sent me some information about that. When I opened my email, he had written to me with the subject, "Urgent!'"

As we discussed over the phone earlier, Ebou Jallow and co. are going ahead with the cyber-terrorism..., hacking Pa Nderry's private email account. Your secret correspondence with Nderry was tampered with and Ebou Jallow for- warded it to the post. Omar, make no mistake..., this is a very serious issue especially the fact that it is you who's been *Freedom* Newspaper's main anchor in Gambia.

From this moment Omar, whatever you chose to do will have a lot to do with your future, your safety in particular. You know as much as I do that this regime will stop at nothing to terminate the life of any independent-minded journalist, you in particular. There's no doubt that these people are gonna go for you and trust me if that happens, you'll be really sorry. They have done it to Deyda, Omar Barrow and attempted to do it to the likes of Ebrima Sillah, Yorro and co. at *The Independent*. Whatever you choose to do from now on, do it wisely and secretly bro.

I wanna suggest that you talk to some Human Rights people in Gambia as soon as possible or even try to go to Senegal for a while. The sooner, the bet- ter. Otherwise, present your case to the US embassy or the British High Com- mission. Have a copy of everything including the letter Ebou Jallow wrote on Gambiapost with regard to your correspondence with Pa Nderry. Talk to them as a matter of urgency and hear them out. Don't ever trust these African em- bassies in Gambia.

Omar, don't tell your problems, worries and anxieties to anyone..., not even your close mates. Don't trust anybody. Do whatever you think is right for you but again make no mistake.... Doing nothing about this will put your life at risk. Always remember that. I have written to the Committee of Concerned

Journalists, and Demba Jawo as well about your plight. I will speak to the people at Chartered Institute of Journalists (CIoJ) and National Union of Journalists (NUJ), both of which I'm a member. Omar whatever you do, wherever you…, stay in touch with me via this email address. I will do anything I can just to make sure you are safe and secure.

God bless you, Sheriff Bojang Jnr.

I read the email repeatedly and wanted to reply to tell him I had escaped from The Gambia but decided against it. First, I had to write to someone. I had a friend, Katia Wagner, a Swedish journalist, who I thought should know about what was going on. She had been my friend for some years now and had visited The Gambia for work and on vacation. I knew she was among a few friends I could turn to in such a desperate situation. I dropped a quick email. I wrote her with the subject, "Danger!"

Hello Katia,
I am in deep trouble with the Gambian authorities. I will forward you some emails and you will understand what exactly I mean. I escaped arrest last night and am now somewhere in SENEGAL. I will give you more information on this as I am really confused and tired at the moment. I spent the night at a car park and now I have nowhere to go but I am searching to see who will harbor me.
Soon
OMAR BAH

I forwarded her the email I had just received from Sheriff Bojang Junior and a few other articles published about the *Freedom* newspaper hacking, so that she would have a gist of what was happening. As I sat in front of the computer, I looked through my bag, and lo and behold, I found a business card of the Gambian woman whom I had met at the Abidjan airport while we were flying back home from the journalists conference in the Ivory Coast. She was Amie Joof, one of the most influential and outspoken human rights advocates against the tyranny in The Gambia. She runs an African- based nonprofit whose offices are situated in Senegal. I rushed back into one of the booths. I dialed her number, and someone answered immediately.

"Hello, it's me Omar Bah…." "Omar! What?" She said.

"I'm inside Dakar now, I don't know where exactly…."

"You have escaped? Oh…, thank God. Oh Omar… thank God you are alive. Please call the shop owner so that he can tell me where you are so that I will

68

come and pick you up immediately."

I called the shop owner to write down the address she was giving me in the Senegalese way of spelling so that any taxi driver I gave it to would understand it. Besides, I did not want to write down the address and possibly spell it: wrongly. I was so relieved that I had found somewhere to go. Before heading out, I rushed back to the computer that I was using and quickly replied to Sheriff 's email:

Hello Sheriff

Thanks for all the support and concern. I have really noticed the seriousness of the whole issue and, accordingly, I left the country late last night and arrived in Dakar at 4am on Tuesday. I spent the rest of the night at the car park. This morning, before writing you, I called Amie Joof, a Gambian based in Dakar, to whose office I am going when I leave the cybercafé. I will keep in touch and am grateful for all the support. I was really confused and undecided at the time you were calling me. Amy Joof's number is: XXXXX, and the office lines are: XXXXX, and Fax, XXXXX. I will get in touch soon. Demba Jawo has not written to me yet but Amie Joof will surely contact him when I reach there.

Omar Bah

9

Grabbing my bag, I rushed out of the cybercafé, jumped into a taxi, gave the driver my little notebook on which the cybercafé owner had written down the address in French for me, and asked him to rush me there immediately. The taxi driver took a glimpse at the notebook and gave it back to me.

Amie Joof had told me to look out for certain buildings and signs as guides to her office. Even though I saw some of such signs, I still confirmed with the driver just to make sure that I was at the actual place. I stepped down and walked up and down a small street in the neighbourhood but could not see the particular address. I asked a storekeeper nearby who pointed at the place for me. When I knocked at the door to the address of my destination, there was a different woman sitting in front of a computer in the lobby. When I explained whom I was looking for, she asked me to sit down and wait for her as she was on her way to the office and could arrive any moment. However, I did not want to sit in some secluded office with a person I did not know. I did not feel safe in there because of my growing paranoia. Therefore, I told her that I was going to sit under some neem trees across the road on the other side of the block. Then I walked away.

I sat on the protruding root of one of the neem trees to wait. The shade of the trees was cool and provided me some sort of respite from the already bak- ing sun. After about half an hour, I saw a woman running across the road, heading towards me. It was Amie Joof. I grabbed my bag and rose up. Her face looked worried, contorted with tension and anguish. She was looking right in my face. In a rush, she beckoned me to follow her. Side by side, the two of us defied traffic and, in a few moments, were inside her office.

I took a seat in the lobby. There was a third woman, Agnes (Pa Louis Thomasi's wife). Amie Joof was still panting from the run to pick me up across the road. The three women stood near where I was seated speechless and worried. They told me that I should have initially waited inside the office, and not by the side of the road. According to them, I was exposed to more danger as Dakar was highly infested with Gambian secret agents who could have kidnapped me and returned me back to The Gambia.

I was speechless myself, terrified and completely worn out. Amie Joof asked me to follow her into her office and gave me a seat near hers. The other two women followed us and stood near Amie Joof. They asked me to be calm and feel safe. The three of them went online and started reading through the postings of my private emails by the Gambian government hacker. The more of the emails they read, the more their faces looked worried. They kept saying to each other, "They would have killed him."

When they were done, Amie Joof turned to me and said she was going to host me in her house in Dakar but that there were two Gambians staying overnight at her house, whom she wanted me to avoid, as she did not want information about my whereabouts to leak. However, she managed to get Demba Jawo, the Gambian that Sheriff had mentioned in his email, to host me for the night.

Before we left for Demba Jawo's, Amie Joof asked me to quickly read a press release of the Paris-based media rights organization, Reporters Without Borders, on the situation of the hacking of the *Freedom* newspaper. I went closer to the screen to read the statement.

Reporters Without Borders
Press release
30 May 2006
.   GAMBIA

Online newspaper hacked, editor smeared, and subscribers threatened

Reporters Without Borders voiced outrage today at an attempt to smear exiled Gambian journalist Pa Nderry (www.freedomnewspaper.com), by hacking into his website and posting a false statement of allegiance to an associate of the president together with the names, addresses, phone numbers and e-mail addresses of all its subscribers, describing them as "informers."

The false declaration of allegiance and the names and details of the subscribers were subsequently published in Gambia in the pro-government Daily Observer, and were immediately followed by an announcement ordering all these "informers" to report to the police.

"This case of hacking is serious and revolting," Reporters Without Borders said. "Not only was the reputation of a journalist besmirched but a large number of Internet users have been put in danger. And it is absolutely astounding that the *Daily Observer* became an accomplice by publishing the list of these so-called informers and describing them as 'subversive'."

The press freedom organization added: "The climate in which Gambian journalists work is totally poisonous. The instigators and perpetrators of this plot must be identified and punished. We reserve the right to be co-plaintiffs in any actions which Pa Nderry Mbai may bring before the British or US courts."

The person who hacked into the *Freedom* Newspaper site on the night of 22 May was a British Telecom client using the IP address of an Internet user based in the British city of Southampton. The hacker erased all of its content and replaced the welcome page with a message purportedly signed by Mbai.

The message said: "I have decided to stop producing the *Freedom* Newspaper as I have pledged an allegiance with my brother Ebou Jallow to join the APRC election campaign." A former army captain, Jallow used to be the spokesman of President Yahya Jammeh's military junta, which took power in a July 1994 coup. The APRC is the president's party, the Alliance for Patriotic Reorientation and Construction.

The message added: "This is a list of the people that were supplying me with information." It was followed by the names and details of all those who had set up user accounts for the site. With help from the US company that hosts the site and from Reporters Without Borders, Mbai managed to regain control of the site the next day and post a denial. His e-mail address was also hacked.

Freedom Newspaper was launched by Mbai at the start of this year. It is very critical of President Jammeh, especially in a column with the byline Bulfaleeh ("Don't Be Bothered" in Wollof), who is portrayed as an anonymous source within the president's office.

Mbai used to work for the tri-weekly newspaper The Point. He was also the Voice of America's correspondent in Gambia. He went into self-imposed exile in the United States after being arrested several times by the National Intelligence Agency (NIA). He was a good friend of The Point co-editor Deyda Hydara, the

Agence France-Presse and Reporters Without Borders correspondent who was gunned down on 16 December 2004.

The privately-owned *Daily Observer* published Mbai's photo on its front page on 24 May under the headline, "*Freedom* Newspaper informers exposed." Calling Mbai the editor of a "subversive" newspaper, it said he had "made a startling revelation of people passing him information against the government, while shifting allegiance to the ruling APRC and shutting down the paper." The next day it published Mbai's US address and phone number along with the names and details of all of his subscribers under the headline "*Freedom* Newspaper Informers list published."

The same day, the Gambian police ordered all those "who continually supplied him with information which he used to castigate and vilify the democratically elected government of His Excellency President Alhaji Yahya Jammeh" to report to the nearest police station within 24 hours or face immediate arrest.

Owned by Amadou Samba, a businessman who supports the president, the *Daily Observer* has been run since October 2005 by Saja Taal, who is its managing director, and Mam Sait Ceesay, its editor. Taal used to be permanent secretary at the education ministry. Ceesay was the president's press officer. They replaced Modou Sanyang and Lamin Cham, who were fired because of their coverage of the crisis between Gambia and Senegal over customs duties. When contacted by Reporters Without Borders, Taal refused to make any comment, saying the matter came under his editor's responsibility. Reached by telephone, Ceesay did not want to answer Reporters Without Borders' questions.

A few days before his site was hacked, Mbai received a message from Jallow, the former junta spokesman. It said: "If you think that you can do whatsoever you want whilst away from the Gambia, then you better think twice... because the impending reaction in the Gambia is going to be very nasty. This is a warning from a brother."

Jallow also forwarded to Mbai a message he had received from someone called William Glass Junior who claimed he was capable of hacking Mbai's site and posting a message on it "to destroy his reputation." Jallow still has not replied to the message Reporters Without Borders sent him on 26 May.

The statement by *Reporters Without Borders* was a good summary of the *Freedom* newspaper hacking crisis. It helped me further understand the extent to which the regime and its associate, Ebou Jallow, were ready to go to harm innocent Gambians based on falsehood and deceit. I shook my head and groaned.

At Demba's apartment, he pulled out his laptop and showed me an article Ebou Jallow had written against the corruption of the president and his government, some years earlier. He wondered why the same Ebou Jallow would now turn around and support the same government he had criticized to the extent of wanting to harm other people. I looked at Demba Jawo, shook my head and groaned yet again. I learned from Demba at night that Katia would call me the next day and that she and Sheriff were coordinating efforts to get me to a much safer place. After eating dinner – a mixture of sour milk, sugar and bread, I spent the night in Demba Jawo's spare room. In the morning, Demba came knocking on the door, burst in, brandishing a cell phone and announcing that I had a call from Katia. I took the phone from him and greeted the caller whose voice sounded hoarse, nervous and tense.

"Omar, you must get out of Senegal immediately," Katia said, adding that it was too close to The Gambia and that my life was still in danger. She said Sheriff had offered to host me in the UK and that she would send money for my ticket to fly there immediately.

I told her that it was a good idea but practically impossible at that time because I would need a visa in order to travel to the UK. She told me that she would get back to Sheriff to strategize and would then fill me in on with their decision. Before she ended the call, she asked me about my family. I told her that I did not know what was happening to them, as I was not able to see or talk to any of my relatives before, I fled The Gambia. Then she promised to seek the help of one of her Swedish friends, Sousou, who speaks one of the Gambian languages, Wollof, to call and tell my mother that I was safe. She added that she would tell Sousosu not to disclose my location to my mother and to warn my mother not to talk about the call to anyone outside my family.

Demba Jawo had breakfast ready for me – an egg sandwich served with tea. While I was eating, he asked me to stay in his bedroom while he went to work. Again, he told me not to hesitate to seek help from the house cleaner if I needed anything. When Demba Jawo left I took my bath and sat in his bedroom. Someone knocked at the door. It was a certain Gambian woman who lived in the same apartment complex and worked with Demba Jawo. We also knew each other back in The Gambia. She was saying hello, and to ask me to calm down and feel safe in the apartment. She told me that the compound was highly secure and that no person was going to enter. She also told me that some of her relatives were downstairs in the living room watching television and that I could join them to get some company. She was also on her way to work.

After about two hours, Ebrima Sillah and Musa Saidykhan on the instructions of Demba Jawo came to take me to the offices of the International Federation of Journalists (IFJ) in downtown Dakar. Ebrima is an exiled Gambian journalist whose house had been burned down by Gambian government agents, while Musa was one of the many journalists arrested in the wake of the March 2006 coup. Up until now, I did not know that Musa was also in exile in Senegal.

PHOTOS

Me as a young reporter at the Daily Observer.

Me (front row, 3rd from right) and colleagues protesting the killing of journalist Deyda Hydara in 2004 by suspected members of the Gambian security.

Me (front row, seated, 1st from left) at the U.S. embassy in The Gambia attending a training on popular culture.

Me (squatting, 5th from left) graduating from a journalism training school.

The abandoned offices of *The Independent* Newspaper which the Gambian regime forcibly closed down. I worked here during my initial years as a journalist.

Me in a dark grey suit, seated (2nd from right), conducting an interview in Senegal while on a trip with fellow Gambian journalists.

Sam-Mbollet village, my home town.

Denton Bridge. I was almost captured here, but by dint of fate, was let go by a soldier who happened to be an acquaintance from earlier years.

80

I used this ferry to cross the River Gambia during my escape journey.
Ironically, (like many public properties in The Gambia) the ferry is named
after the dictator's home town of Kanilai.

The walls of the fence of the notorious Yundum Barracks showing the picture
of Dictator Yahya Jammeh. Behind these walls was where I encountered my
first arrest and torture experience by soldiers who kicked and hit me with gun
butts and later jailed me in a tiny mosquito-infested cell.

Omar Bah declared wanted

See story on page 2

Om Bah

Bah declared wanted

Cont'd from page 1

The Gambia Police Force has issued a press release to say that following Pa Nderry Mbai's declaration that he has decided to stop producing his on line Freedom Newspaper and revealed his sources of information. Mr Omar Bah, News Editor of the *Daily Observer* Newspaper, is presently at large. Mr Bah is required to report himself to the nearest police station with immediate effect. The release warns the general public not to provide any shelter for Omar Bah and any person found wanting in this regard would be charged for aiding and abetting. The release therefore solicits the cooperation of the general public.

Me in the headlines of the *Daily Observer* as a 'Wanted' man.

10

The three of us sat in the lobby of the IFJ offices to wait. The office was highly air-conditioned, a respite from the hot and humid weather outside. Sillah took a seat in front of one of the computers while Musa sat next to him, looking on. Both of them were reading the latest news articles on the Internet written about my saga. They were very attentive, and I could notice the movement of their lips as they read silently. At some point, Musa stopped looking at the screen to look at me. He gaped at me and said, "You are the luckiest man on Earth".

Musa was right. I could not imagine how I could have possibly survived the brutality of the Gambian security had I been arrested. If I had not been 'the luckiest man', I would have been killed by now; or I would have been facing torture. In such a terribly humid weather, I could not imagine being continually tortured in a tiny mosquito-infested cell of the notorious Mile 2 Prisons. That prison is so terrible that it is nicknamed Africa's Hell on Earth – the dictator mockingly refers to it as such when he detains his opponents, real or perceived. He sometimes says that Africa's Hell on Earth is his Five-Star hotel accommodation for his opponents.

As I thought about Musa's remark, a staff member of the IFJ announced to us that the director would soon see us. Meanwhile, many journalists who were attending an international conference on media in Dakar at the time came to show solidarity with me when they heard I was at the IFJ offices. In addition, a Senegalese journalist, Sheriff Faye, who used to work at a radio station in The Gambia that the regime had closed, also visited me at the IFJ office and gave me his contact information and asked me not to hesitate to turn to him if I needed help.

Finally, Musa, Ebrima and I were ushered into the office of the IFJ director, Mr Gabriel Baglo. He looked distraught and tired.

Ebrima updated the director on my ordeal and those of other Gambian journalists, including Musa. As if on cue, Musa removed his shirt to show the scars from lashes and bayonet wounds he had sustained while in detention. The director gawked at Musa's festering wounds and shivered in disbelief. He asked us all to calm down and be extra careful while inside Senegal. He told us that he would be issuing a statement about the "grave situation" in The Gambia. Throughout the meeting, I was silent. I was too fatigued and emotional to talk. The three of us returned to the lounge. Ebrima and Musa each sat in front of a computer. There was breaking news coming in from The Gambia. More people were being arrested in connection with the *Freedom* newspaper hacking. One of them was my former editor, Lamin Cham, who was arrested purposely because of me. In one of my emails that the hacker circulated online, I had mentioned Lamin, even though the reference to him had nothing to do with my work for the *Freedom* newspaper or the stories I was writing, he ultimately became one more victim of the regime.

Ebrima was reading an alert dispatched by Sulayman Makalo, the assistant editor-in-chief of *the Independent* newspaper, to the international community and human rights organizations. I stepped forward and stood by Ebrima to read the message.

> Lamin Cham, the BBC stinger in The Gambia has been arrested by the security forces. The reason for Mr Cham's arrest is not known and his whereabouts unclear.
>
> However, the *Daily Observer* news editor Omar Bah is nowhere to be traced for three days. His co-workers who fear that he might have been arrested, said they last heard from him when he reportedly had a problem. It is not known what problem he had, and his mobile is switched off.
>
> Omar is a personal friend of Pa Nderry Mbai, editor and publisher of the US based on-line *Freedom* Newspaper.
>
> Sulayman Makalo
> Assistant Editor-In-Chief
> *The Independent* Newspaper

After seeing the Sulayman Makalo message, the three of us became jittery and feared that at the rate the government was rounding up people indiscriminately, many more journalists could fall prey and we decided to alert those whom we thought could be in harm's way to flee the country. One of such journalists was Ousman Darboe who when Ebrima called said he had never reported for the *Freedom* newspaper but was told nonetheless to be on his guard for any eventuality.

I took a seat in front of the computer and went online to read what had been written about me. There were many stories and commentaries suggesting that I was missing, dead, or at large. I checked my emails. Katia had written to me.

Omar, take it slow!!!!

Don't make any quick decisions. I will forward Bojang's letter to our union national office. Let me send you some money with Western Union—let me know where to, and how your status is. Also if there is a phone number.

Get back to me!

-Katia

Sheriff had also replied to the email I wrote to him when I had arrived in Dakar.

Omar,

I'm so relieved to know that you made your way out. The matter is damn serious which is why it's so important for you to leave. Demba Jawo dropped me an email too to let me know you're with him out there. Omar, what we gonna do now is to wait patiently and see what the authorities will do or say about you. I'm sure something is gonna be printed or even a press release about you. Once that happens, we'll take things from there. I can assure you that you won't be at the losing end in the scenario. Let's just give them till the end of this week towards mid-next week to see what's gonna come up.

Stay in touch with your family and mates and please let me know whether anyone's been in trouble with regard to your whereabouts. We'll move on from there.

For your info, I had a phone call from one Katia Wagner in Sweden, claiming to be your friend. We spoke at length about the issue and we'll keep talking to see how best u can leave Dakar. But we'll have to wait for the authorities' reactions.

I'll ring you later on.

Regards, Sheriff

Sheriff also forwarded me an exchange of email conversations he and Katia had had the day earlier. When I read those emails, I was humbled to see how much effort they were both doing about me from their end.

Hello, Mr Bojang,
Good to speak to you. I know you are a very important person to Omar and I'm glad he turned both to you and me. Please let me know as soon as you hear from him.
All the best,
Katia Wagner

Hi There,
Thanks for contacting me and being so concerned about Omar's welfare. He's at the moment in Dakar, Senegal. He's staying with Mr Demba Jawo who's currently working in Senegal. He dropped me an email to tell me that Omar's with him. You can contact Omar there at XXXXX or XXXXX (mobile). I'll forward to you the email from Mr Demba Jawo and Omar himself. Let's keep in touch about this issue and help Omar out. My house number is XXXXX.
Regards,
Sheriff

Hi again,
Thanks for your email. Let me know when you speak to Omar himself. I will call tonight or tomorrow. As soon as he has decided he wants to leave Dakar I will send him the money through Western Union. Let us stay in contact!
Regards,
Katia

I stepped away from the computer after reading through all these emails. I felt I needed a little time for myself to reflect deeply about my life. I did not want to feel too emotional by thinking too much. It was getting late and dark outside. The IFJ was working on its press statement. By now, Amie Joof and Agnes had joined us at the IFJ office. (Agnes is the wife of Pa Louis Thomasi whom I first tried to call without success when I was looking for a place to stay. Agnes also worked with Amie Joof. Her husband was on a trip outside Senegal which explained why I could not reach his phone when I called the day earlier). By now, several media organizations and human rights organizations around the world had issued statements about the abuse of journalists and human rights in The Gambia.

The two women sat next to me and promised that they would do everything possible to help me out of my situation. Agnes gave me a plastic bag with clothes. It was a selection from her husband's wardrobe. The clothes were three pairs of trousers, two shirts, two T-shirts and a kaftan set. I thanked her for her generosity but she asked me not to, as according to her, it was her duty to stand by me in my difficult moment and that I should see all of them around as family.

Baglo showed everyone the draft of the statement he was about to issue and invited comments from all those present. As a result, the final draft mentioned the names of journalists who had been released and those still in detention, and then condemned the act in the strongest possible terms. For security reasons, Ebrima suggested that the release should be vague about Musa and me, which was couched thus: *"...because of these threats and the arrests of their colleagues, two journalists have fled the country. Their whereabouts are not yet known."*

Before we left, the IFJ office gave me and Musa some money as their contribution to our upkeep while staying in Dakar. Then we all left. I was not returning to Abu's house this time around. All the five of us – me, Ebrima, Musa, and the two women headed to Amie Joof's house.

While we were still stuck in the traffic, Amie Joof told me about a certain Professor Kwame Karikari, the head of the Media Foundation for West Africa (MFWA) in Accra, Ghana. According to Amie Joof, my presence in Dakar was timely in the sense that the professor was also in the city at the same time attending a conference. Amie Joof said she would reach out to the professor and suggest possibilities of relocating me to Ghana so that I would be safer and farther from The Gambia. "Ghana is a good place. They are nice people. Maybe you can even go to school there," she said.

I nodded but said nothing. I was not sure I knew what to decide or do about my future. However, I was sure of one thing – all my friends in Senegal and everyone helping me meant the whole world to me, and I knew they would do anything to help give my life a new meaning.

We reached Amie Joof's home at about ten in the night, ate and then Musa and Ebrima left while I settled in for the night. When Amie Joof showed me the room I was to sleep in, as though she were reading my mind, she said:

"The room is safe and the gate to the compound is also locked. Do not fear anything. Be comfortable and have some rest. Nothing will happen to you here."

I nodded and thanked her.

11

On the morning of Thursday, June 1, 2006, Amie Joof knocked on my door and said, "Omar, you have a call from Katia."

I took the phone and spoke with my friend who was calling from Sweden once again. That was the second time she was speaking with me since I fled The Gambia.

She told me Sousou was able to reach my mother on the phone the day before and told her that I was safe. She added that she would send me some money for my upkeep and asked me to be strong in these trying times as I would surely come out of them a better person. I was ecstatic to learn that my family had known that I was safe and told Katia how grateful I was for her support and encouragement. Then Amie Joof and I left for her office, where I browsed the Internet to catch up on the latest developments about the situation in The Gambia. I saw that one of the country's leading newspapers, The Point, had run a story about my escape:

Observer News Editor on the Run
BBC's Lamin Cham Detained
Thursday 1st June 2006
By M. Justice Darboe & Alhagie Mbye

Omar Bah, News Editor of the *Daily Observer* cum Secretary General of the Gambia Press Union, is on the run, reports say. Mr Lamin Cham, a former editor-in-chief with the *Daily Ob- server* and now the BBC Banjul-based correspondent, was also in detention at the NIA Headquarters in Banjul as we go to press. RVTH Senior Communications Officer, Malick Mboob, now sacked, was also in detention at the time of writing this story.

The reason(s) for Omar's decision as well as the detention of Cham and Mboob could not be immediately verified but are believed to be linked to the ongoing investigations on the *Freedom* Newspaper.

I had also received an email from one Yankuba Dabo. He was the one who was with Sheriff when he called me on the night of my escape. I had briefly spoken to Yankuba Dabo in one of Sheriff's phone calls that night. Therefore, his email was a sort of a follow-up.

Dear Omar,
It is good to know that you are safe and well. You keep strong as you always are! The system is trying to break us down but they do not know we are getting strong and stronger, we are bonded in this struggle and we will not be defeated. I'm finishing university next week so I'm kind of in the middle of exams at the moment but once I'm done we will be in touch more. Be strong Omar if one thing Jammeh has succeeded in doing is making brothers and that's what we will be forever.
This is my email address so let's keep in touch.
Yanks

Yankuba's email was both touching and encouraging. When I read it, I began to believe that really, all freedom-loving people around the world were with me.

We returned home around twilight. The sun was hanging over the tiled roofs of Dakar toward the Atlantic Ocean. It had cast a reddish ray on the city so much so that everywhere looked red. When we entered the house, I sat on the sofa in Amie Joof's living room while she settled down inside. Then something happened— something that was perhaps one of the most frightening things to happen to me after my escape. Ebrima Sillah stormed into the house with his eyes sticking out.

"Bureau Chief" he said. He had begun addressing me "Bureau Chief" because the hacker revealed in my private emails that I was the *Freedom* newspaper bureau chief in The Gambia. I could not wait to have him talk. He was striding toward me, as if some apparent danger was pursuing him. "Have you heard the news? Have you heard what happened?" I could not guess what it might be but I trembled in anticipation of what he was going to tell me. I had wanted to get up, but I was stuck in the sofa. I was still, and all I could do was to stare and wait for Sillah (he is generally addressed by a mere Sillah by his acquaintances). *What if it is my family – my wife, siblings, par- ents or any other relative that had been harmed? Oh God. Help me.* Amie Joof had overheard Sillah's rumbling and rushed out of her bedroom.

"I was just listening to Radio Gambia news. The Government of The Gambia has declared you 'WANTED'! Omar, this is getting very serious. Amie Joof I think we need to act fast. This man's life is in real danger!"

I froze.

The room was quiet. Their eyes were fixed on me. I tried to look around the room but the little energy I had was not enough to raise my eyebrows. I tried to think. I could not. I wanted to say something, but I couldn't either. Amie Joof came to my rescue. She sat on the arm of the sofa beside me and caressed my head and face with her tender hands, reminiscent of how my mother used to cuddle me when I fell sick with malaria as a child.

When it was eight at night, we all stayed glued to the television for the Gambian national news relayed across the Gambia Radio and Television Services. Thanks to technology, Gambian television could be accessed across the world. I saw two of my media colleagues Chief Ebrima Manneh and Ebrima Baldeh covering some event at the State House. I wondered whether I would ever see them again. Other announcements followed, concerning arrests of high profile people including a National Assembly member, Mrs Duta Kamaso who was expelled from the ruling party.

Then came the big story of the day. In a solemn voice—the tone of someone who did not seem to like what he was saying—the news presenter announced that I had been declared a wanted man and went on to read the full text of the press release issued by the Gambian regime about me:

> ... Mr Omar Bah, News Editor of the *Daily Observer* newspaper, is presently at large. Mr Bah is required to report himself to the nearest police station with immediate effect. The general public is hereby warned not to provide shelter for Omar Bah and any person found wanting in this regard would be charged for aiding and abetting. The cooperation of the general public is therefore solicited.

I could not tell what exactly came through me. And I could not express the depth of sorrow and cold stream that ran through me. I could not just imagine the drama unfolding in my life. I wanted to think, but I could not. I leaned back on the chair and remained still. Sillah was furious. He was fuming and was talking as if he was going to kill the president right there and then. The room was full with people now. They were all talking and bemoaning the dictatorship and the killings and tortures going on in our country. From time to time, I was inclined to add a few words to the discussion, but would let go. The people in the room were not only angry because of the 'WANTED' declaration against me, but they were even more fearful for my life.

Amie Joof heaved a sigh of relief – perhaps relieved that I was still alive. However, I could see more anger in Sillah's face – perhaps angrier that a sadistic and murderous tyrant had subjected me to such misery.

I wanted to go to bed, but Amie Joof would not let me be all alone in my room. She was afraid that the dictator's secret agents could spirit themselves into my room at night and abduct me. She instead suggested I spend the night on a mattress on the floor of her bedroom. She did not want me to be alone so that if we sensed trouble, we both could raise the alarm together. I stood in the middle of the room, one hand crossed over the chest while the other cupped my chin. I did not know what to do first, or how to respond to her, but out of sheer instinct, I told her that I would try to sleep in my room—that I would be vigilant. Then we all dispersed.

I went to bed pessimistic about everything—that I could be caught and harmed and probably murdered; my wife and the rest of my relatives were still in danger. I was not sure whether the dictator's secret agents had found my location. I did not also know what might have already happened to my relatives. By now, I was convinced that I was not entirely safe, and that it was just a matter of time before I faced my fate: death. I tried to sleep, but it was hard. When I closed my eyes, I would see assassins inside the room whispering and pointing guns at me. Sometimes I would jump up and look around the room but would see nothing. Sometimes, I would peer out of the window and the tiny openings on the side of the door to see whether someone was hovering around.

I needed help. I could not continue like that. There was a lot of tension inside me, as if something was going to explode from inside of me. I was distraught. I pulled my tape player and put on my headphones to listen to my ethnic Fula violin music. At least there was some noise—it sounded like some noise—but it helped stabilize the situation somehow. Soon, I drifted into sleep.

On June 2, 2006, which was my fourth day in exile I received yet another call from Katia who asked to know how I was keeping and urged me to remain strong. Since I did not accompany Amie Joof to her office, I went with a young woman living in Amie Joof's house to a cybercafé nearby and luckily found both Sillah and Musa there, surfing the Net.

I saw that the *Daily Observer* and *The Point newspapers* also ran the press release in which I had been declared a wanted man. In addition, many media and human rights organizations around the world had written extensively about me, with most stating that I was missing and imploring the Gambia government not to harm me. I also saw an email from one Ibrahima Diallo, a supporter and fan of my weekly interview column, based in Guinea. He wrote:

> Hi Omar, I'm very surprised. Now what can I do for you? I have seen on the Observer that you are wanted by the police, please take great care of yourself. Thanks a lot.
>
> Your Brother Ibrahima

Also, I received an email from Sheriff alerting journalists and human rights advocates about the gravity of my situation. The alert titled, 'A JOURNALIST IN DANGER!' was circulated around the world. In that statement, he emphasized the danger I was in:

TO WHERE IT MATTERS

May I first of all introduce myself in a bid to give you a clue that out of experience, I know the subject matter on which I am writing. My name is Sheriff Bojang Jnr. I am a 25-year old Gambian Journalist currently based in the United Kingdom. I worked at *Daily Observer* Gambia Ltd as a Freelance Reporter, then a Senior Staff Reporter, Columnist, Sub Editor and Head of Political Desk. I resigned from Observer in July 2001 as a result of editorial interference from senior officials of the government of The Gambia. I then joined *The Independent* newspaper (Gambia) as a Senior Reporter and also corresponded for the BBC African Service briefly before I left The Gambia for a journalism programme with Reuters in London, UK. As at now, I am a member of The Gambia Press Union, Committee for Concerned Journalists (CCJ), Chartered Institute of Journalists (UK), National Union of Journalists (UK) and Royal Society of Literature (UK).

Dear compatriots and friends in the media, I feel it is incumbent upon me as a concerned Gambian journalist to inform the world about the current unfortunate and disturbing plight of Gambian journalists and journalism, in the hands of the dictatorial and heavy handed regime of President Yahya Jammeh. Recently, *Free- dom* Newspaper, an online newspaper which was created to investigate and publish key political and administrative issues about

President Yahya Jammeh and The Gambia Government was hacked by criminals. The online newspaper is headed by Mr Pa Nderry Mbai, a former senior journalist at The Point and also Voice of America's Gambia stringer. Mr M'bai's life was threatened in Gambia and he eventually left for the US where he now lives.

Though the hacking investigations are still going on, it is widely believed that some Gambia government agents were behind this criminal act. The cyber criminals tampered with private email accounts of Mr Mbai and his colleagues at *Freedom* Newspaper which gave them access to all their correspondences with the outer world. The list of all the subscribers and so-called informers of the online newspaper was sent to Daily Observer, a pro-government newspaper, by the hackers. *Daily Observer* went ahead and published all the names of subscribers and referred to them as "informers who have been giving information to Mr Mbai to vilify the democratically-elected government of President Yahya Jammeh". This was followed by an urgent press release from The Gambia Police Force, ordering all those on the list to report to the nearest police stations for interrogation or face arrest and prosecution. People across the country have been arrested since then while others reported to the police voluntarily. So the whole episode is being treated by the government, through the police and National Intelligence Agency (NIA) as a kind of treason.

Dear friends and comrades, the two main journalists at the center of this political witch-hunt are Mr Omar Bah and Mr Lamin Cham. Omar Bah, in his mid-twenties, has been the News Editor at government-monitored *Daily Observer* and also the Secretary General of The Gambia Press Union. On many occasions, the management of Observer threatened him with the sack simply because his beloved father is a village chairman of one of the opposition parties in the country. This further gave the security authorities an excuse to monitor Omar's day-to-day activities with keen interest.

After supplying *Daily Observer* with the so-called informers list, the hackers sent Omar Bah's private email correspondence with *Freedom* Newspaper editor to various public websites and government institutions in The Gambia. This email correspondence which must have been read by the Gambian authorities, proved beyond reasonable doubt that Omar was the author of all the sensitive and well-kept presidential and government secrets published by *Free-*

dom Newspaper. These stories range from a soldier being tortured by the authorities for alleged coup plot to the health of the president's mother.

My dear colleagues and friends of the media, this unfortunate event, most importantly, put Omar's life at risk. He went into hiding within the country as security agents went around looking for him. He was then able to make his way out of the country. For security and safety reasons, I cannot, at this time, say where Omar is currently but I know out of experience that he is not 100% safe there. About two hours ago, I rang a couple of journalists in Gambia who both informed me that armed military personnel and plain-clothes security agents have been in and out of Omar's office at Observer and other places looking for him. There remains a roof of insecurity hanging over his head. If the authorities can arrest and detain the mere subscribers and readers of the *Freedom* newspaper, what cruelty in the world can't they do to Omar, the man behind all the stories the government described as "evil and threat to national security"?

Another victim is Lamin Cham, the current BBC Banjul stringer. He was arrested early yesterday by security agents and has been detained incommunicado since then. In one of Omar's emails to *Freedom* newspaper Editor, he told him "people like Lamin Cham have been so supportive of me". The state interpreted this as Cham's involvement with the online paper. So one can come to the conclusion that Cham was arrested because the authorities believed he is also a collaborator with *Freedom* Newspaper. At the time of writing this letter, Cham was still in detention and was not charged with any crime.

Dear colleagues, may I refresh your memories that in December 2004, Deyda Hydara, a veteran Gambian journalist, was a victim of horrendous murder. In a similar horrendous act earlier, the house of Ebrima Sillah, former BBC Banjul correspondent, was set alight and he almost lost his life during the attack. It was the same story with *The Independent* and Radio 1 FM when they got their offices set on fire by trigger-happy pro-government criminals. None of these culprits were ever arrested or brought to justice.

On behalf of Omar Bah and Lamin Cham, and all other troubled journalists in the hands of the intrusive and obtrusive regime in Gambia, I wish to call on all of you to join forces and help them out by putting pressure on Gambia government. They are in serious

trouble and they need us to act as soon as possible. Only time will tell what cruelties Cham will succumb to while in detention or whether Omar Bah is safe where he is at this juncture.
Looking forward to your support.
Sheriff Bojang Jnr.

When I got home, I occupied myself by reading Tom Clancy's *Clear and Present Danger* and watching Nigerian movies. Later that night, Amie Joof, Agnes, Sillah and Musa all agreed that I had to be taken out of Senegal to a much safer place, preferably Ghana.

12

On the afternoon of Sunday, June 4, 2006, Amie Joof organized a lunch retreat in her house and invited all my friends in Dakar. She also invited Professor Kwame Karikari who had already been informed of my situation. The lunch was meant purposely to have the professor come to Amie Joof's house to strengthen our efforts in getting me out of Senegal.

The house was filled with people. Demba Jawo, the man in whose house I first slept when I arrived in Dakar, was in. Sillah, and Musa and his wife were present too. Agnes and her sister were in. There were two more women. One of them was a former secretary of a slain Gambian journalist who was injured when the journalist was killed in a drive-by shooting. She had since been living in Senegal. The other woman heads an organization in Senegal that advocates for human rights and freedom. In fact, the human rights advocate donated some money to me when she arrived as part of her organization's contribution. The professor was the last one to show up.

In the course of the windy discussion centred mostly on the lamentable situation in The Gambia, Professor Karikari suggested that the gathering should get copies of newspapers that published the story in which the government had declared me wanted. According to him, I might need them in the future or for posterity. That was not going to be easy because anyone caught showing the slightest interest in my case could be in trouble in The Gambia. Agnes's sister, who was about to travel home to The Gambia, but would return to Senegal after some days, offered that she would take the risk to try to get at least one of such newspaper copies. According to her, a relative of hers normally received newspaper supplies, and all she needed to do was to look through the stack and get the paper without anyone noticing it. However, everyone advised her to be extra careful in doing that, as even the border security could arrest her for attempting to leave the country with such a paper. If caught trying to smuggle that paper out of The Gambia, the government could harm her on the suspicion that she had information about me.

The professor opined that the dictatorship era in The Gambia would certainly be swept away by the new wave of democratization in West Africa. He cited his native Ghana, Nigeria, Mali and Senegal as good examples of countries where dictatorship or self-perpetuating rule were becoming obsolete. "So it's only this buffoon (referring to Gambian president, Yahya Jammeh) who is still doing this thing." He urged Gambians to come together to effectively challenge the tyranny. Some of the guests including the professor and Demba Jawo left later in the evening.

As we were about to break up for the night, Abie's cell phone rang. It was her husband, Pa Louis Thomasi, calling from Monrovia, Liberia. Everyone was silent and looking at her.

"What?" Agnes said. "Is that what he did?"

She was sitting on the floor. Whatever her husband was telling her from the other end of the line could not be good news. She looked bewildered. One of her hands cupped her chin, while the other supported her on the floor where she sat. She was silent for a while. It seemed she was listening carefully. However, the rest of us were also eager to know what Pa Louis had told her.

When Agnes finished talking on the phone, almost everyone simultaneously wanted to know what her husband had told her. She told us that her husband had just seen on the Net that Pa Nderry M'bai had disclosed in his paper that I had found sanctuary in Dakar, Senegal. She said her husband was upset that this disclosure could give me away. Everyone else was upset as well, wishing that Editor M'bai had exercised self-restraint.

I was confused. I turned to Musa who was sitting next to me on the sofa and said to him in a slow, low tone, "I don't know what is going to happen to my life."

Musa also looked confused. He did not respond, but he looked agonized. He looked down and in the other direction. The room was now as silent as a graveyard. I stared down blankly at the floo for a while. Everyone was looking at me. Shivering, I rose and walked past everyone down the corridor and went into the little room where I used to sleep. I threw myself on the bed. Though I was tired, I could not sleep.

Both Amie Joof and Agnes came into the room and sat on the edge of the tiny bed where I was lying. It looked like the group had sent them to ease my worries and fears. Agnes opened the discussion with occasional chipins by

Amie Joof. They assured me that they would rather die than let anyone harm or abduct me and then reassured me that I would get my life together once again and move on to a level that would make my current predicament seem like a mere dream. They talked on like that for a long time, but all I did was to stare at the ceiling and occasionally steal glances at them. I promised them that I would be calm.

It was now over a week since I escaped from The Gambia and I learned later from Amie Joof that Lamin Cham, the BBC correspondent in The Gambia arrested shortly after my escape for his alleged connection with me had been released. At times, I felt like I was living a life replete with nothingness – at least so it was – full of ambiguities and uncertainties. For me the whole drama looked surreal, struggling to come to terms with the fact that this was actually happening to me.

However, I kept myself busy by browsing the Internet at Amie Joof's office. On the morning of June 7 when I arrived at Amie Joof's office, Katia called again from Sweden. Her call was brief. She just wanted to know how I was faring. I saw that so much had been written about my escape but before reading them, I decided to check my emails. I had received a short email from a former colleague who was now living somewhere in Europe.

> Hi Omar,
> Boy please try and send me a number so that I will call you as soon as possible. I was told that you are in Dakar. I want to give you contacts there.
> My tel number is ###. Call now

I was grateful for the efforts of the writer of the email. But apart from my friends, Katia and Sheriff, I did not respond to anyone else's email. I was going to stay like that for a while. Besides, I did not have to call the person because I already had a place to stay.

There was another email from one Kanta, which made me sad. Kanta is a half brother of my father with whom I grew up in the same compound in Sam-Mbollet until when he was about twelve years old and I eleven. Then we were separated when his father died. His mother, being a second wife, moved to another village with her children. The separation deeply caused us emotional trauma. The two of us had hoped to go to circumcision together, and to continue to live together for the remainder of our childhood. The two of us reconnected later on in life and became best friends once again. It was through one of my visits to Kanta's village, during his elder brother's bride welcoming ceremony, that I met my wife, Teddi. In my ethnic Fula culture, your father's relative – brother or half brother addressed you as their son or daughter – not nephew or niece. Only your mother's relatives address you as their nephew or niece. Therefore, in the somber email below, Kanta did occasionally refer to me as 'son'.

Hello my dear son and best friend in life. Since I heard what has happened, I could not be in peace. I cannot eat and sleep the whole night. I keep thinking of you, where you should be by now.

It seems I'm not alive. My life without seeing you is zero. No second, minute and hour passes without my mind focusing on you. My heart keeps on knock- ing while I think of you. It is very sad and confusing. Everybody is calling me and asking me about what happen but I always say I don't know. Why? Be- cause they know how close we are.

Boy we could not see each other and cannot talk to each other but I know you are also thinking of me too just like I'm dying here of too much of sadness. Just have the faith and know it's God's will. It's a tribulation brought to you by God and one day it will be finished and you will come back to your home- land and be with your family. For sure, Allah will do that. I am here praying for you so that Allah will help you. I cannot forget you in my life and will not leave your family members. Last Saturday on the 3rd of June, I went to your mother so that she could be relieved when she saw me. I really talked to her so that she could have the faith on Allah, and let her just pray for you and take out charity for you. And she really takes my advices. She will do as I told her. I will be going there from time to time and give her whatever I have until Allah will come to your aid and release you from all these problems.

Be careful and be watchful. Boy, you really make me lonely. I miss you, my friend. As I'm writing to you, tears are rolling down to my face. You are my son and my best friend in life. We have done many things together and when I think of that I cry. I am finished! I am praying to ALLAH so that we see each other before we die! Amen. I wish you all the best in life.

This is your friend, and everything in life. Be safe and be blessed. Bye, with tears.

As most emails I have received of late, he also did not sign off with his name. People were afraid and tried to be careful in every way. While I was reading the email, tears flooded down my cheeks uncontrollably. I had not cried so painfully like that for a long time.

I was now confined to Amie Joof's house. I was not leaving the house or going anywhere near the gate. There was a likelihood that I might relocate to Ghana. However, while the arrangements were being made, I was to be fullyprotected which meant that I should not go out of the house. Accessing news was not easy for me now since I was always indoors and thus scarcely went online to read about developments back home. Nonetheless, I was able to re- ceive news from third parties such as my friends, and from Amie Joof. That way, I learned that Internet access to the *Freedom* newspaper within The Gambia was blocked on Sunday, June 11, that an anonymous letter writer had claimed responsibility for the blockade. The same letter writer, they said, criticized the *Freedom* newspaper staff including me as being rebellious against the Gambian regime and thus, deserved punishment. In addition to the blockade, there had not been any updates on the paper for a while. Many believed that the hacker might have done more harm to the website. However, about a week later, the *Freedom* newspaper editor resumed posting again and explained that the break in posting was because the website was being overhauled.

I also learned that one Lamin Fatty, a Gambian journalist, had been released from illegal detention by the regime. That was a great relief because that particular journalist had been under detention for more than two months.

I continued to live in that way for several days. However, I was not completely in the dark as my friends always gathered in the house in the evenings to keep me company. During one of such gatherings, Musa informed me that there were rumors that one Musa Jammeh, a notorious thug in the presidential guards, had been reported missing, but he later resurfaced and continued torturing opponents of the regime. Amie Joof also informed me that Buba Baldeh, a former minister in the previous government and one-time managing director of the *Daily Observer* newspaper, had fled The Gambia on accusation of involvement in an alleged coup – he was now also in exile in Dakar.

13

It was Thursday morning June 22, 2006. From the rays of sun filtering into the house, I could tell that it was going to be a bright day. I had been confined inside Amie Joof's house for two consecutive weeks now. When I went to the bathroom and looked at my face in the mirror, the image I saw looked like a stranger to me. My hair had grown long and rough. My facial hair had also grown and was strewn all over my face. The bones in my face were protruding. I had grown extremely thin. My eyes were very red and bulging, and always itchy. Generally, I looked as though I had just stepped out of the Stone Age. Despite my awful appearance, Amie Joof decided that I should accompany her to the office, where I learned I was going to Ghana on Sunday June 25, 2006.

At first, I did not know what to say because I didn't know what to expect in Ghana. Besides, I hardly knew anyone in Ghana. Yet Ghana seemed to be my best alternative given my grave situation.

As part of my travel arrangements, I should be physically present at the airline office in order to get my ticket. Thus, the following day, on Friday, June 23, 2006, I went with Amie Joof to her office again. Agnes was at the office that day too. They asked me to wait while they arranged for me to get to the airline office. Later, Agnes told me that her husband had called to say he was willing to take me to the airline office. His office was not far from where I was. Thus, he asked Agnes to put me in a taxi that would take me right to the front of his office. She told me to be extra vigilant because of the risk involved.

The airline was close to Pa Louis Thomasi's office. He walked me down there and we quickly picked up the air ticket. As soon as we got the ticket, we returned to his office. We were there until he finished work, later in the evening. Pa Louis and I grabbed a taxi and he took me back to Amie Joof's house where I was staying. There, Amie Joof and all my friends were around, chatting in the living room. They all had received the news now.

Later that evening, Pa Louis and Agnes suggested that I go home with them for me to see their home before leaving the country. Among all my friends in Dakar, they were the only folks whose home I had not visited yet. I had been to the homes of the other people at least at some point during my stay. Besides, they were the ones I most probably would have stayed with had I gotten Pa Louis on the phone on the first morning of my arrival. I was therefore honored to have the chance to visit and to sleep over at their home. The three of us hopped into a taxi. The traffic was congested, and people were selling things on each side of the road. There were many children dressed in tattered rags holding tins. They were begging for food and money. Their faces were as bare as their feet. I thought about them and felt sorry for them. I was quiet throughout the journey. Every now and then, Pa Louis Thomasi or Agnes would ask me whether I was okay. I could not participate in their discussion as I was busy looking at the scenes in the streets.

Africa is all the same. You see similar scenes of poverty and deprivation in The Gambia too. Like my own country, Senegal also has paradox of opulence co-existing with penury. Some of the streets looked very modern with beautifully lined streetlights and nicely dressed people with beautiful cars. Such were the very rich people. In contrast, there were streets laden with chaotic situations—honking buses and taxis galore. In addition, like the children – the young beggars – people looked raggedy and extremely poor, malnourished and bereft of the national cake. I do not know when African leaders will see what the suffering people are seeing. This is not fair.

When we reached the entrance of their home, Pa Louis Thomasi asked us to walk fast so that we could quickly get into the building. He said his neighbourhood was not safe in the sense that Gambian secret agents were suspected to live in one of the mansions nearby. He said some of the occupants of the said mansion pretended to be staff of the Gambian embassy in Senegal. However, in reality, they were agents and could potentially be spying on his house. We flocked together quickly and within seconds, we were already in the house. Pa Louis made sure the doors were properly locked before we settled down.

Pa Louis Thomasi and Agnes had a beautiful apartment with admirable furniture. Before I sat down, Pa Louis Thomasi showed me the guest room and the bathroom. He also gave me toothpaste and brush, a towel and a pair of slippers. The three of us stayed for a long time in their living room, eating, watching TV and discussing Gambia. We stayed so late that Agnes had to leave the two of us in the living room to go to bed. By the time Pa Louis Thomasi and I retired for the night it was already two in the morning.

The IFJ gave me some money in addition to what they had already given to me. The latest gift, according to the IFJ, was meant as my pocket money while in Ghana. I told Pa Louis Thomasi that I wished to buy a travelling bag with the money I had on me.

In the late afternoon, Pa Louis Thomasi took me to the downtown Dakar area to buy a travelling bag. It was a quick trip. As soon as we bought the bag, we changed the remaining money into American dollars because it is convertible, and thus could be used anywhere. Then we returned to his house. By the time we got there, it was already late. It was time for me to go back to Amie Joof's house and the three of us set out to go. However, before we left, Pa Louis Thomasi surprised me with a gift of a dress suit with a pair of pants and a white shirt. In addition, he also gave me a towel, toothbrush and paste. I was so touched by his and his wife's generosity. I felt it was not necessary because when I initially arrived in the country, Agnes had given me enough clothes from Pa Louis Thomasi's closet. I was exceedingly grateful. I left my country without any belongings except my workbag and today, the couple had given me so many clothes that I felt I was home. In addition, Agnes gave me a copy of the *Daily Observer* newspaper that her sister was able to smuggle out of The Gambia for me. It carried the story where the government declared me a 'WANTED' man. According to her, she closely coordinated with her sister. In fact, they used the code name 'Adel' for me while the sister was back in The Gambia. In that way, the two were able to communicate by telephone without worrying about who might be listening to their conversation.

The three of us headed to Amie Joof's house. When we arrived, she and my other friends, Sillah and Musa were chatting in the living room. It was a very special Saturday evening; it was going to be my last night in Senegal. There-fore, everyone hung around until late that night. We talked about the usual topics: the dictator back home; the missing people; those who are tortured; the illegally detained; the bad economy; the degradation of the living standards in our country and all the vices of the regime. At the end of the gathering, we consoled each other; we assured each other that things would eventually get better and then dispersed.

There are certain days in one's life that one never forgets. Sunday June 25, 2006 was a special day in my life. I was about to leave for Ghana. Like the fateful day I escaped from my country, this day also meant a lot to me.

However, I was disturbed about the uncertainty in my life. I had no idea what I was going to do with my life in Ghana. All I knew was that I was going to get some respite given the distance between that country and The Gambia. I did not know whether I would be living in Ghana for the rest of my life. I could not imagine living a life that seemingly had no future or sense of direction. My current predicament had changed my life – it made me value freedom more than ever before.

Amie Joof called Demba Jawo on his mobile phone. According to her, even though he already knew about my going to Ghana, it was proper for us to speak with him. We both spoke with him. We expressed our gratitude once again for his unflinching support and for letting me sleep in his house when I first arrived in Senegal.

He said he would be coming over to see me before I left for the airport.

Amie Joof and my friends in Senegal had organized a send-off lunch. Before our friends would gather, Amie Joof asked a nephew of hers who was about my age to take me to a nearby shop to buy body lotion and deodorant. From there, he would quickly take me to a barber's shop nearby in order to cut my hair. She gave him money for us to use. As usual, Amie Joof told us to be extra careful and not to take chances.

It was a quick trip. When we got home, Amie Joof's house was filled with people. Everyone smiled when they saw me and complimented my clean haircut. I smiled and greeted them all. Amie Joof asked me to proceed to my room to pack so that when it was time to depart, I would not be rushing. A little girl – a five-year old granddaughter of Amie Joof's followed me into the room. She started begging me not to go. The little children in the house had grown very fond of me. "Uncle Omar. I don't want you to leave," the little girl said, as I packed my things inside my traveler's bag. She looked sad, but I calmed her down by promising to return.

Packing was easy because I had little luggage. I soon joined the rest of the gathering in Amie Joof's living room. All eyes were on me. I wore a slight smile with a nebulous expression. I said little that day. I could see in some of the faces of my friends that they were sad – or perhaps more worried than sad. Demba Jawo did not stay long because he was working that particular Sunday. He gave me some money and asked me to use it as pocket money. Before he left, he advised me to be steadfast and careful while in Ghana and hoped that life would be better for me there. We shook hands and he left.

My flight was scheduled to depart at 4:00PM. However, Pa Louis Thomasi called Air Senegal to confirm the time as he said the airline was fond of changing its schedules. As expected Pa Louis Thomasi found out that my departure time had indeed changed to 6:00PM. I grinned when he said that. I looked around the room and everyone seemed happy about that because it meant having more time with them. For security reasons, my friends did not want me to wait at the airport for long, and thus, confirming the departure time beforehand was important.

Amie Joof had a plan. She said that since I had two more hours, she would help me talk to my family back home before leaving. That would be the first time I would be speaking with them since my escape almost a month earlier. That was so generous and thoughtful of her. My inability to talk to my family had really taken a huge toll on me. It was therefore a great relief when Amie Joof told me about the possibility of talking to them.

There was just one problem though – Amie Joof could not call from her cell phone as the Gambian regime might possibly trace her number. We suspected the Gambian regime might have tapped into the phones of my family members. Thus, I had to call from a tele-center, which was a few streets from her house. The others would wait while Amie Joof took me to the tele-center. They would be very quick conversations. The idea was for my family members to hear my voice and be reassured that I was indeed alive. I wanted to call – my wife, mother, and father only. To any of those, Amie Joof would call first and make sure that the particular person we were calling was the very one on the phone. Then she would hand me the phone. None of us would mention our names or the names of the people to whom we were talking.

When we arrived at the tele-centre, Amie Joof dialed my wife's number. I was at once nervous, sad, and happy. I hoped I would not break the rules that Amie and I had laid down before coming to the tele-center.

"Hello, how are you?" Amie Joof said in the Wollof language.

My heart was beating fast. I was eager to take the phone and hear my wife's voice. Then Amie Joof added, "We are calling from a distant place and cannot identify ourselves. Hold on for somebody." Then she passed me the phone.

"Hello!" I said in a low but tense voice.

"Hello... Hello! How are you? I Thank God! I hope you are fine and safe. I miss you. I am so happy to hear your voice..."

"Me too," I said. The ridges on my forehead pulled together and mobbed vertically in between my eyes. Below my eyes, I felt like someone was pulling some flesh and hurting me. I felt dizzy, tense, and exhausted. I gnashed my teeth hard and willed myself not to cry. "I am glad to know that you are fine. I am also fine and healthy. I am lucky to have good and wonderful people around me who have taken all kinds of risk to help me. Do not worry about anything. I am okay."

I could hear how loud she was breathing, perhaps even sobbing. However, I did not ask because I did not want to stir emotions. We assured each other to stay safe and be careful and hoped that such ordeal would all be over soon.

"I am relocating to another place today. I will endeavour to call more often

105

as soon as I am settled in my new location," I said. "I love you," she said.

"I love you, too," I said and handed the phone to Amie Joof who ended the call.

The next person we called was my mother. As soon as she received the call, Amie Joof went through the same ritual as she did with my wife – we were calling from a distant place; and we were not going to identify ourselves. When I said "hello", my mother answered in a rather nervous tone. Some children were making a lot of noise in the background.

"Wait... let me rush to the bathroom in order to be able to talk.... Hello!"

I could tell that she was running.

Then I said, "Hello! This is me. How are you? I am fine and safe.

I am so happy to hear your voice."

She lowered her voice and responded in like manner. She said she was happy to hear my voice and to know that I was safe. She prayed for my safety, ease of life as a wayfarer and good health.

I told her what I had told my wife, and then we called my father. He was in Barra, hanging out at his friend's shop. As soon as Amie Joof handed me the phone to talk to him, he broke down in tears. He said he never thought he would talk to me in life again, as he thought the government had killed me and that he was overjoyed knowing that I was alive and safe. As soon as we reached home, I shook hands with everyone and headed out of the compound. Amie Joof, Sillah, Pa Louis Thomasi, Agnes, Musa and his wife accompanied me to airport. Some other people in the compound joined us but they were stopping at the place we were picking a taxi. I was beautifully dressed in the dress suit that Pa Louis had given me. Someone held my bag for me. As we walked along the street, I kept looking back at Amie Joof's house. It was a nostalgic moment, but I stayed strong and walked on.

While we waited for a taxi, someone expressed concern about my safety at the airport, but Amie Joof allayed our fears by disclosing that she had a friend at the police station at the airport with whom she had arranged to stay on the lookout. When we reached the lounge, I was the only one allowed to enter for checking-in while the rest waited. Musa gave me his cellphone to use while they waited for me. As soon as I passed the door, Amie called me and asked that I kept the line on so that they would hear the background noise and be able to ascertain whether I was safe or not. I did as she advised. As soon as my bag was checked-in, I went back to them for a final farewell. I could see that they were sad. I had an immigration form that I had to fill out. Sillah volunteered to bend down so that I used his back for a desk to complete the form. When I first arrived in Senegal, Demba in whose house I first slept had bought me a Tigo cellular SIM card. However, I never used it. The few people I wanted to talk to knew Amie Joof's number and used to call me through her. Thus, I did not need the SIM card then, but I needed it now. Amie Joof asked me to insert it in my phone so that she would call me and have my line open when I returned to the airport waiting room. Amie Joof told me that some airport security officers were watching over me, and that I should not fear anything. I looked at all of them, one after the other. None said a single word. It was tough to part company with them, but I had to go. I shook their hands and hugged them. "Thank you for everything," I said as I hugged them one after the other. As I walked back toward the waiting room, Amie Joof reminded me that she was going to call me soon and that I should keep the line open. I nodded, and as soon as we reached home, I shook hands with everyone and left. Before passing the door to the waiting room, I looked back once again. My friends were still standing at the same spot, looking at me.

Amie Joof called my cell phone and stayed on the phone with me. My departure time was delayed a little longer and that made Amie Joof nervous. She kept praying over the phone that I left the country sooner than later. She told me that she and her friends were planning to return to the airport if the wait continued. She was tense and disappointed about the delay.

Finally, when I boarded the bus that transported the passengers to the plane, she was jubilant. I could hear the chorus of relief rambling from the voices of the rest in the background. By now, they were back at Amie Joof's living room and keeping each other company there.

I stopped for a while as I boarded the plane, looked back at Senegal, and entered the plane — a new chapter in my escape journey; in my new life as an exilee; as a wayfarer; and a wanderer. I took a window seat and kept talking to Amie Joof on the phone. It did not take long before the plane departed. When the plane started taxiing around and the announcement came that cellphones and electronic gadgets should be switched off, I informed Amie Joof and told her with certainty that I was safe and out of Senegal. She was silent.

"Thank God!" She said when she finally broke the silence. "Please say thank you to everybody on my behalf once again. I cannot say how grateful I am to them all," I said. "I will. I will surely tell them."

"And for you…" I hesitated and stopped. I was short of words and did not truly have the best words to say to her. "And for you…" "For me," she said. "I am your mother. Please do not say anything. I am your mother and exhausted." I gnashed my teeth hard and willed myself not to "Bye."

"Okay."

"Thank you. Bye."

She ended the call. Tears ran down my cheeks. I cried so hard that the front of my shirt was all wet.

107

14

My trip to Accra, the capital city of Ghana, took about three hours. The Media Foundation for West Africa had initially suggested in one of their emails to Amie Joof that I should be looking out for someone with a placard bearing my name as soon as I walked out of the arrivals lounge in Accra. However, Amie Joof suggested that the name of MFWA should be on the placard instead of mine, because a Gambian could be among the arrivals, and possibly see my name and give the game away. My flight had a brief stop in Abidjan, Ivory Coast and landed at about ten thirty at night at the Kotoka Airport. 'AKWAABA', was the first thing I noticed as I entered the airport terminal. I would ask about the meaning later on, as my first lesson in learning a Ghanaian language and was told it meant 'welcome'. After collecting my baggage, I followed the crowd in a procession toward an exit gate. There were so many taxi drivers outside scrambling for passengers. "Master. You need a taxi?" They chorused. I kept walking, looking at either side of the pavement.

In addition to the drivers, there were also many other people displaying placards bearing the names of people or organizations. Standing in a prominent position was a young man with the placard bearing the words: 'MEDIA FOUNDATION'. I immediately waved at him. He came over to me and shook my hand.

"Omar, Welcome." He said. "Thank you," I said.

He took my traveller's bag that I was dragging. "Why did they keep changing your flight?"

I smiled, giggled and said nothing.

He motioned that I followed him. We walked to a taxi park across from where we were standing and hopped into one. In one of the numerous emails that Amie Joof had received from the MFWA, I remember seeing the name of the young man who was going to pick me up, but I could not remember what the name exactly was. My closest guess was Peter.

"Are you Peter?" I asked.

He and the taxi driver seemed to be acquaintances. They both laughed before he said, "Me? No Richard".

It sounded "Richid" to me. "What?" I said.

He repeated it twice before I could figure out his exact name. Our accents were different and this was a first lesson to both of us that we needed to listen attentively to each other before we got used to the differing accents.

The driver revved the engine and drove away from the parking lot. Before getting out of the parking lot, he swiped something at a post so that the cross bar in front of us lifted up to allow the car passage.

"Wow!" I said to myself. I was awed. Ghana looked like an advanced country. Apart from the card swiping, their airport was well built and gave the impression of a rapidly developing country. After a short drive into the city, the taxi pulled over at a little hotel called King David Hotel. Richard got my bag out of the taxi and asked me to follow him inside the hotel. It seemed that he had done all the necessary reservations before I arrived. We proceeded straight to my room on the second floor. He asked me to feel safe and comfortable and that he was going home but would come back to the hotel first thing in the morning to see me.

The following morning, I woke up early. I took a shower and put my clothes on. Out of the window of my room, I saw a woman bending and sweeping with palm-tree brooms in the compound courtyard next to the hotel. That reminded me a lot about The Gambia. I watched children run around the woman just like my siblings and I would do in our compound courtyard when I was a child. Like The Gambia, there were rusted corrugated iron roofs on some houses, too. I looked at the bustling street to the right and saw people walking in either direction. There were little shops and stalls and it looked like people were busy buying breakfast. "Africa is all the same," I said aloud.

Much to my chagrin, Accra is a huge city. There were huge highways and beautifully paved roads lining the bustle of modern structures. There were so many restaurants and bars on the sides of streets. There were so many people and everyone seemed to be busy running some errand. I felt a surge of pride and ecstasy to be in Ghana, the land of Kwame Nkrumah whose name is folklore to every African child because of his visionary leadership in weaning Ghana out of colonial rule, the first sub-Saharan African country to do so. It

109

reminded me of my middle school days. My school, Berending Middle School, was categorized into four houses named after great African leaders. I was in Nkrumah House for the three years and was its head in my third year. Thus, the little thing I knew about Kwame Nkrumah had inspired me a great deal and I had always loved Ghana since, and always wanted to go there. Ironically, here I was in the midst of Accra, the capital city of Ghana. "Life is a flux", an editor of mine once wrote in a highly acclaimed essay. In as much as I had fantasized about visiting Ghana someday, I never thought it would indeed be possible – not the least under the circumstances I came there. Nevertheless, such is life, and thus, I took it for what it was.

As Richard and I walked along the streets of Accra, I marvelled at the beautiful roads and modern structures. Businesses were booming, and so many activities were going on. "This is a very big city," I said. "I don't think I will ever get to know my way around."

"Accra? Accra," he said, laughing. "You will know here very soon. Wait and see."

At the MFWA offices, I met a fellow exiled journalist Siriki Diabate, fondly known as Nico, a short form of Nicodemus who had fled from the Ivory Coast a year earlier. I liked him immediately because he was witty and positive, always looking at the sunnier side of life. Because he had gone through experiences similar to mine, we became kindred spirits. He relished calling me "Omar Bah From Gambia". He was also bilingual, fluent in both English and French. I learned that he was the one who used to translate press release about my ordeal into the French language for the MFWA.

One day Siriki and I went around town to see some places of interest. We walked past Joy FM. Siriki pointed at the building to our right and said, "That is the radio station that we always listen to when we are in the Media Foundation office. That is the one you heard us listening to today. Now let us walk this way. I will show you the Accra motor way."

"What is that? Is it a highway?" I said. "Yes! It is the motor way."

We were now standing near the Accra Motor Way. The highway was wide and big, with so many cars on its many lanes. I confessed to Siriki that I had never seen such a well-constructed highway before. "Ghana is doing well," I said.

"Omar Bah From Gambia, you have not seen anything yet. I will show you Accra." We turned left and walked toward the Ghana Telecom. There were so many buses and mini buses. Young men brandishing money were running up and down wooing passengers to join their vehicles. Siriki and I shoved them away and managed to walk through the bus chaos. "This is what is called

Tro-Tro in Ghana," he said to me.

"This is interesting. In The Gambia, we call similar minibuses *Gele-Gele*."

We climbed a high and wide overpass in order to get into a nearby open market. From there, we walked through some traffic congestion. There were so many people that I thought there was a festival or some sort of occasion, but Siriki told me that it was just a normal day. I was beginning to understand why people say millions of people live in Accra. We crossed a few more roads. We were standing next to the iconic Kwame Nkrumah Circle.

"In The Gambia, we call these kinds of spots, 'Turn Table' instead of 'Circle'. Wow, is this the center of Accra?" I said. "Center of Accra…? Omar Bah From Gambia, you have not seen anything. I will take you to other parts of the city. You will see more things," he said.

I returned to my hotel room and switched on the TV. It was music time. Many of the singers sounded gospel-like, which soothed my frayed nerves. One of such was the song *Maforebo Nwom* by Abigail Apenteng. It looked like it was a big hit in the market as the stations kept repeating it. Ghana had many signs of progress. A good impression of that was the vibrancy of the country's media. When I went to the MFWA offices during the day, I saw so many newspapers that I could not remember how many they were. Some of them carried headlines and stories that were very critical of the government and would have warranted an arrest or killing of journalists in my native Gambia. The radio station that we tuned at the office, *Joy FM*, was also a vibrant radio with up-to-date and interesting news bulletins. Moreover, here I was, in the middle of my hotel bed, switching from one TV station to another. I was not sure how many stations they had, but I counted four channels. I shook my head and wondered when The Gambia would emulate great examples like Ghana.

I continued my new routine—going to the MFWA in the morning, do whatever I could to help with their work, interact with the people there and return to the hotel. I was allowed to attend their staff meetings. Professor Kwame Karikari spoke mostly at such meetings. He asked me to help the coordinator of the Network of African Freedom of Expression Organizations (NAFEO), the organization's project in fighting against press freedom violations in The Gambia and around West Africa. He also asked me to help in general work around the office. I was glad to be given the opportunity to keep myself busy.

15

Living in Ghana was quite an improvement on my previous solitary life in Senegal; however, I was still plagued with uncertainties, not knowing what the future held for me. Taking the advice of Amie Joof and my friends back in Senegal, I did not disclose much about my family when I was in Ghana. Thus, I did not talk much about relatives, especially my wife.

A few days after arriving in Ghana, I called and spoke with my wife, Teddi. Neither of us mentioned the other's name because we did not know who might be listening. She sobbed over the phone telling me how miserable her life was and how most of our friends except for a few had abandoned her. She however told me about the enormous support she had received from both my close relatives and hers.

I assured her that the whole predicament would be over some day and that we would live happily together again, when it was all history. When I put down the phone I wept as I had never done before because I missed Teddi so much and longed for the day when we would see each other again. I could not believe that we were separated from each other after two months of marriage.

I met Teddi during a bride welcoming ceremony at Sare Marry when I was barely twenty-one years old and was struggling to be self-sufficient as a rookie reporter and a law student at GTTI. What attracted me to her was her demure nature. She is fairly tall, fair in complexion, and slim and walks with such grace that I sometimes tease her that she is like a female sibling of mine because she shares many physical traits with my sister, especially the way she tilts her head while walking. She always smiles which illuminates her oval shaped face.

In the course of the three-day bride welcoming ceremony, I got closer to Teddi and even protected her against the taunts of her age group, who suspected that both of us were up to something.

On the second night of the bride-welcoming ceremony, an open dance was organized in the courtyard of the compound where the groom lived. Three pairs of boys and girls were to first step in the middle of the circular gathering to officially open the dance. I was among the three boys called upon and, not surprisingly, I was paired to dance with Teddi, who hid herself somewhere because of her shyness. As a result, I was paired with someone else, but as we held each other's hand and waist, and swung this way and that, I wished I was doing it with Teddi. At the end of the ceremony, Teddi and I had become acquainted with each other. She had told me more about herself and her village and I in turn told her about myself; my education; and journalistic work. Throughout, I encouraged her to take her studies seriously. Before we parted, we promised to remain good friends and to keep in touch.

With the help of my friend Assan Sarr who hails from Sare Cherno where Teddi was schooling, both Teddi and I were able to exchange letters, as telephones were rare in rural Gambia. At some point when I did not see Assan any more, my communications with Teddi broke down. I felt sad because I had never before had a female friend that close. I yearned for the day that I would see her again. I could still visualize her soft, gentle, radiant face and braids woven from the front to the back in straight lines.

It was not until around mid-2003 when I saw Teddi again when I attended another bride welcoming ceremony in the same village. When my friend Kanta and his girlfriend Rubbie saw me at the ceremony, they went in search of Teddi and brought her to me. She had grown in both size and height, and appeared much lighter in complexion. Even her face seemed different and I had to stare at her for a while before I could connect it with what she looked like a few years earlier. However, she said she was unhappy with me because I had suddenly broken contact with her and left her miserable for such a long time. I explained why I had not been in touch and then reassured her that my life without her was meaningless. My explanation and apology seemed to mollify her as she smiled and snuggled up to me.

A few days after speaking with Teddi, I had also called my mother and father. Just like my normal phone calls now, the conversations were short and brief and none of us would mention each other's names. Those were my most miserable moments – not being able to speak freely to people who mattered to me most. Even so, I was glad that we could at least hear each other's voice.

111

I also called my two friends, Sheriff Bojang Junior in the UK, and Katia Wagner in Sweden. I had occasionally called Amie Joof in Senegal too. I gave them my new phone number in Ghana. They all gave me words of encouragement and support. I felt strong and uplifted whenever I spoke with them. After all those phone calls, during my first weeks in Ghana, I felt more confident and relieved. I felt somewhat settled in my new home – Ghana.

My new life in Ghana was as simple as that – call my family briefly when I could, go to the Media Foundation offices and return, interact with a few people – and such was life. I continued to monitor events back home in The Gambia. I occasionally heard that people, including my colleagues, had been arrested and tortured and some even reportedly missing. I learned that government security forces had arrested a former colleague of mine at the Daily Observer, Ebrima Chief Manneh, whom no one had seen since his arrest. Worse still, the government kept denying having him in their custody. I felt sad because I could imagine the cruelty those sadists were inflicting on him. It made me even more scared of my own security in Ghana as the Gambian government could still kidnap me and smuggle me back to The Gambia. I shivered whenever I thought of such a scenario.

Around the beginning of July – the first week or so – the miserable life I was living in was exacerbated by a terrible development. While at the Media Foundation offices, I had strolled down to the Ghana Telecom vicinity to eat lunch at the street-side stalls. I was feeling hot, exhausted and dizzy. While I was eating a plate of fried rice and chicken, I looked at the newspaper kiosk nearby. The Ebony newspaper headline 'GRUESOME' captured my attention. I stopped eating and went over to read the story, which told of the brutal beating to coma of three people purported to be dealers in international currency inside their hotel room at King David Hotel. I almost fainted.

If such a crime could be committed while I was staying there, then I was no longer safe. The person who had just served me food noticed that I was acting strange and offered to help but I waved him away. I rose and walked toward the Media Foundation offices. One of the things I had wanted to do at the Ghana Telecom neighbourhood was to repair my cell phone that had been acting up, but I was no longer thinking of that now. I had more serious issues to deal with. At the Media Foundation, I sat in a little corner, brooding over my life, wondering why trouble seemed to be following me wherever I went.

Just then, one of the staff on the second floor, Daisy, broke into my thought. "Omar! Are you okay?" She said.

"Yes! Why?"

"Did you see the newspaper?"

I was happy that they had also seen the story because it meant they would do something about my predicament. I told her that I had seen it and that I was worried about my safety in the hotel.

In a solemn voice, she assured that I would be safe and nothing bad would happen to me in Ghana.

On Wednesday July 12, 2006, the Media Foundation moved me out of King David Hotel to some blocks down the same Kokomlemle neighbourhood. It was a room created from cardboard walls on one side of a veranda. I would share a common bathroom and toilet with the other tenants in the compound. I was happy and comfortable because I felt safer there than being at the hotel. The other tenants did not know my story but were nice and hospitable and were always asking about my wellbeing. Besides, the people that helped the Media Foundation get the room for me lived in the compound next door. They had assured the Media Foundation that they would be my guardians and that they would help me adjust to my new neighborhood and take good care of me, which they did. They are among the most caring people I had ever met since I left my country. They were always concerned about me and made sure I had food to eat.

I was however confused by their names. The woman who got the apartment for the Media Foundation was called Penny. She had a shop at the corner of their house next to where I was living. One day, as I was passing by to go to my house, I saw her dumping some garbage in the garbage can by the street.

"Hello Penny, how are you?" I said.

She smiled and said "How are you? But I'm not Penny."

"I don't understand? Are you not the one who helped the Media Foundation to get my room for me?"

I knew she was generous because on the first day that I moved to my room, she gave me a carton of water, and a broom for cleaning my room.

"I know….It's my sister O…, my twin sister, Penny." "Oh, you guys are twins? You look so identical.

"I am Kakra. She is Penny."

I nodded. "I am Omar…, Omar Bah."

However, Kakra told me that she was a little bit bigger than Penny in weight and that as I got to know them more, I would notice more distinguishing peculiarities between them and would not have trouble telling them apart. In addition, while Kakra ran a tailoring shop, Penny owned a drink store, which was adjacent to the tailoring shop at the corner of their compound. Therefore, the stores would also be some ways of distinguishing them. The area of the Kokomlemle neighbourhood in Accra that I was now living was farther from the Media Foundation offices than the hotel I had stayed in before. Unlike The

Gambia where most of the topography is flat and levelled, Ghana had some hilly slopes that I found fascinating. I had to go up a slightly hilly slope before descending a little bit again when going to the Media Foundation office. On weekends or in the evenings when I was home, I would sometimes stroll up the hill to go to a cybercafé or to use the sides-street calling stalls to talk to my family back home. It was never enough calling my family as we had all missed each other so much. Teddi always told me how lonely and distressed she was while I said the same thing. Nevertheless, the good part of it was that we always encouraged each other to stay strong and have faith.

16

When I was in The Gambia, I had planned to attend the congress of the International Federation of Environmental Journalists (IFEJ) in Stockholm, which I had to abandon when I ran into trouble. The organizers nonetheless kept sending me emails about my participation. I did not respond to the emails because I did not see any reason in responding to such kind of correspondence – I was in deep trouble and was preoccupied with how to be safe and not to participate in conferences. Besides, apart from my passport that was in my bag when I was escaping, I had not done any feature stories on environmental issues in The Gambia that I could present. So even if I could travel, I felt the best use I would be there was to be a mere number – but not much. Notwithstanding that, the organizers kept reminding me about it and one of them said that I could share my experiences with them when I arrived in Sweden. That got me hooked and thus began working with the organizers on my travel arrangements.

The Media Foundation supported me and helped me with the necessary documentation for my visa application. On the day before my travel to Sweden, one of the officials at Media Foundation asked me whether I would be applying for political asylum once I arrived. "Asylum? No! I will not apply for political asylum there," I said.

I would really have loved to do so if I had the way to do so. Because all I was looking for was a safe place, where I could settle down and feel safe. However, the main reason why I was not going to do so was that I did not want to let down the organizers of the conference. I decided that I would return to Ghana and face whatever fate had for me. Before going home that day, the Media Foundation gave me some cash, as pocket money.

Before heading to the airport, I sent a quick email to Katia to inform her about my visit to her country. I was elated that I was visiting her country because she had stood by me through all this difficult period and had been occasionally sending money to me and my family. She lived in a city far away from the capital, Stockholm, where I was going.

After a stop in Amsterdam, I joined a connecting flight to Stockholm Arlanda airport. It was my first trip outside Africa. I was still battling with depression and thus did not pay much attention to the exciting new things I was seeing for the first time in my life. In both places – in Amsterdam and Stockholm, the airports were much bigger, fancier and more sophisticated than any airport I had seen in Africa. Both airports looked like whole cities to me.

At the airport in Stockholm, I saw an African woman and I thought she might be one of the conference attendees. I greeted and asked. She was indeed one of the attendees. I felt happy and relieved because now I had someone to go with to the hotel, and eventually to the conference place. We joined the bus to a place called T-Centralen where we would transit with train to our hotel. It was going to be my first time to enter a train.

In as much as I had marveled at the exceptional standards of buses and road quality, I was mesmerized by T-Centralen – a state-of-the art structure. It had beautifully constructed underground facilities and stores and all sorts of stair belts. It was beautiful and shiny and busy. I thought about the dilapidated structures of under-development in Africa, shook my head and just hoped that our leaders in Africa would start understanding what leadership really meant and improve the social conditions of their people.

We were late. The participants were at the conference venue but some of the organizers were at the hotel to take us to conference venue. I was extremely tired. I had missed my sleep because of the difference in time and because of the long journey. I had hoped to have a nap at the hotel but that would not be possible since the conference was already on. I just dropped my travelling bag, headed to the lobby, and joined the person who was there to take us to the conference. As I expected, I did not make a presentation during the congress, but I had the opportunity to hear the wonderful presentations of some participants. I was also glad to have the opportunity to share the story about my current predicament with my fellow participants at a personal level and in small groups. The organizers were interested in my welfare and future and offered to help. When they asked me what kind of help I would need, I told them that I would like to relocate to any English-speaking country in the Western Hemisphere because I did not feel safe in Africa.

While in Sweden, I got an email from Katia who asked for a number on which she could call me. I emailed her the number of a fellow conference participant who had offered to let me use his phone whenever I needed to. She called immediately.

"Omar," she said, her voice tingling with excitement. "I can't believe I'm speaking to you right here in Sweden."

She had me speak with her two little daughters who knew me very well too as they had all visited The Gambia several times before. They were glad that I was safe; and that I was visiting Sweden. Katia told me that she could not come over to see me because where she lived was far away from Stockholm. She told me she would be calling regularly to talk to me and that her friend, Sousou, (who called to inform my mother a few days after I escaped) who was in Stockholm would visit me. I was happy to know that Sousou was in town because she was such a wonderful friend of mine as well. I had met her through Katia in The Gambia in late 2004 and she briefly practiced the Wollof language with me. She had been in The Gambia, then, for some time learning the Kora musical instrument, and Wollof.

Sousou visited the hotel to see me. She looked sad but also relieved that I was alive. She kept emphasizing that she was so happy to see me. I thanked her for calling my mother during the most trying moments in my life and generally for standing by me. My new friends at the conference could not believe it when they saw that Sousou was fluent in an African language. When I also told them about her Kora talent, they pleaded with her to come and play for us at the hotel. She said she would have loved to play for us, but she already had a couple of concerts lined up.

Sousou visited at the hotel regularly throughout my stay. She normally brought a phone card that she said Katia had bought for me so that I would use it to call my family in The Gambia. She became acquainted with some of my new friends and she accepted to join us one day for our conference dinner at a restaurant in town.

Sousosu also had a friend, Helena, whom I had also met. Helena had visited Sousou in The Gambia when the latter was learning the Kora instrument. I had met her too and we all became good friends. Helena's interest was in line with journalism, and she was interested in doing some work with me just as I did with Katia (whom I had met a little earlier). Helena's visit to The Gambia was short but we had the opportunity to conduct a joint one-on-one interview with a controversial guest for my weekly column, *Bantaba*. After Helena returned home to Sweden in December 2004, we communicated for a short time afterwards and then cut off contact. However, that was soon going to end, as Helena was going to call her for us to talk.

"Hello…, hello Omar…. Hello!" I could feel how excited and nervous she

117

was. We were both evidently happy to talk to each other for the first time in nearly two years. During our conversation, she asked me about one thing in Sweden that I noticed was different. It was a difficult question. I felt like she was giving me the taste of what I normally did to my interviewees during my one-on-one interview sessions since I was reputed to ask tough questions.

"Time..., time," I said.

The question was hard because I was on my first trip in Europe. Everything looked better than The Gambia. For example, I had never entered a train before. I had never entered a place like T-Centralen that would lead me below ground level. In addition, the infrastructure—the roads, the beautiful and clean city, everything—was wonderful to me. Nevertheless, since I had to mention only one thing, 'Time' stood out for me. In The Gambia, punctuality is a challenge. By contrast, in Sweden, time was obsessively worshipped; the time to go to the conference, to bus, to train, to dinner, and everything—is right on the dot.

My interactions with Swedish friends made me relive my days as anchor of the *Bantaba*. Apart from my other tasks as a journalist, *Bantaba* had been the main focus of my discussions with Katia, and later Sousou, as they both helped analyze it with a view to making it more engaging. I had started *Bantaba* nearly two years before I met them.

One of the first guests on *Bantaba* was Pa Sallah Jeng, then Mayor of the capital city, Banjul. Mr Jeng had an enthusiastic support base in the city at a time when many had lost faith in the democratization process of the country. After The Gambia's presidential elections in 2001, the main opposition United Democratic Party boycotted the subsequent parliamentary and local government elections. During the presidential elections, the government had used both state security and party thugs to harass and intimidate the opposition. As a result, many opposition supporters were seriously tortured, imprisoned or sacked from their jobs. An opposition supporter, identified as Ousman Ceesay, was shot dead by a soldier in broad daylight when security personnel and ruling party supporters attacked them at a campaign rally in the Tallinding suburb of Serrekunda city, just two days before the elections. In addition, just about a year before the parliamentary elections, ruling party thugs armed with machetes had ambushed an opposition convoy touring the country's provincial areas. In the ensuing mayhem, several opposition supporters sustained serious injuries and had most of their cars destroyed. A ruling party supporter died in the mayhem, resulting in the arrest and detention of several opposition leaders. As a result, the main opposition felt harassed and believed elections in the country would not be free and fair. Thus, they boycotted the 2002 parliamentary and local government elections. A few politicians, however, decided to contest various seats on the ticket of other opposition camps or as independents.

Pa Sallah Jeng was one of such independent candidates. To everyone's surprise, he was able to overcome the ruling party machine— with all its intimidation, harassment and monetary inducement—to win the mayoral seat of the nation's capital. That was one of the most humiliating moments for the ruling party. In my interview with him, he came across as a courageous man with a social conscience.

Another guest was Nyimasata Sanneh Bojang, the first Gambian woman to win a parliamentary seat. She had also held important posts in the country, under the previous government. Before her breakthrough, women generally played second fiddle in politics in the country by mostly helping in organizing political rallies, clapping, dancing, cheering, and voting. Her political triumph broke that jinx. When the current President, Yahya Jammeh, came to power, she came close to the corridors of power yet again, by being Minister of Health and subsequently as a nominated member of the National Assembly.

Yet another guest of mine was Alieu Kama Badjie, who was a minister in the deposed government. In the wake of the 1994 coup, soldiers young enough to be his grandchildren arrested him together with his colleagues and subjected them to all sorts of maltreatment. During my interview with him, he recounted how he had "precipitated" with sweat, dehydrated, and suffered to the extent that he thought he would lose his life.

In conducting my interviewing, I applied a formula that was to become popular in the country. My formula was simple: soft in the beginning with questions intended to provide background about the interviewee and the like, and generally to 'break the ice'. I asked the tough questions in the middle, and ended the interview in a softer tone. The purpose of ending the interview in a soft tone was to soothe frayed nerves, some sort of goodbye to an interviewee who might have already been aggravated. It also served to show I was human, not an enemy out to destroy him or her by exposing their dirty linen in public by asking such tough questions. I always wanted my interviewees to understand the ardent difference between questioning and making mere statements, and the latter was not in my business.

Because of my tough line of interviewing, many government officials perceived to be corrupt declined my interview requests, while some dragged their feet before accepting my interview requests. I soon became a target of threats and intimidation by people who felt that my interviews where insulting to them.

In contrast, the ordinary person in the street enjoyed my interviews. When, for example, I interviewed Sana Sabally, the former army captain who, with current president, Yahya Jammeh, seized power together in 1994, the reaction around town was inspiring. Sana had just been released from a nine-year jail term. Before he fell out with the military council that headed the country at the time, he was its second in command as vice chairman. However, about six months after they took over the country, some of his colleagues arrested him and jailed him together with another top soldier in the council. Like the rest of the military thugs who were ruling the country, Sana was a beast feared all over the country. Thus, when he was released from prison, the country was eager to hear from him. I was the first journalist to sit with him for a one-on-one discussion. It was tough on him because I asked about all the rumors and conceptions that people had about him including torture and harassment of Gambians while he was in power. The interview was so long that it was published in a two-part series.

Just as some people loved the *Bantaba*, many others complained that I was "rude," "ill-mannered," "uncultured," and "un-Gambian". Most of them said I was practicing Western type of journalism, which they said had no place in Gambian culture. According to them, Gambian culture did not permit a younger person questioning authority especially leaders, and older people. Some would call to insult me, while some would send me poison-pen letters, which were published in the paper's OP-ED page.

At some point, the critique on my column was so strong that a national debate ensued with people for and against the 'Omar Bah's type of journalism. Both sides regularly wrote commentaries in the media to argue their points. I never responded to the critics during the debate about my type of journalism. Even though I had an opinion, I felt I should stay back and enjoy the drama. However, I was compelled to respond to one of such writers with the last name 'Sarr', who claimed to be a journalism student in America. I then categorized her as a professional critic, not just another reader. I expressed my disappointment with her for three reasons: the fact that she was a journalism student; the fact that she had had the opportunity to see advanced type of journalism in America; and that she ought to know better as she had seen much more of the outside world.

Despite the threats and controversies, I never budged in my style of journalism and line of questioning. I continued to interview and demand answers from public officials and politicians. Some were becoming more aggressive as if they had been enthusiastic about the controversy surrounding my column. While some abused me, I never retorted; I simply focused on asking my questions and subsequently would publish their tantrums verbatim. One such politician called me a "backward person" for merely asking him a question he did not like. The interviewees' relatives sometimes went on the offensive, as in the case of the niece of a certain parliamentarian whom I had asked whether he was an alcoholic.

Another controversial interview I had was with a minister in the previous government who had a love child with an expatriate civil servant. The media noise that ensued was deafening.

When the majority leader in parliament, Baba Jobe, suddenly fell out of favor with the dictator and was jailed, most of his close associates distanced themselves from him. They did this to avoid the wrath of the dictator. I interviewed one of such former friends of the jailed majority leader. He was also a parliamentarian. He had been one of the closest friends and associates of the jailed leader yet he was among the first to make public comments to disown him. I titled my interview with him, "Friend or Judas?" One of the most interesting parts of the interview was that my interviewee could not explain why he had hitherto been an ardent supporter and defender of the former majority leader. He could also not explain why he was so desperate to disown his friend at a time when his friend needed him most.

Another of such persons that I interviewed was the new majority leader in parliament, following the jailing of his predecessor. Like most top politicians in the country, the new majority leader had already formed a personality cult around him. When I turned up for my appointment to interview the new majority leader, his office was full with his fellow parliamentarians from the ruling party. As he motioned me into the office, I overheard one of the people in the room mutter, "What is he doing here?"

My interviewee, however, laughed it off and said, "Omar Bah. What kind of journalist are you? No recorder, no notebook, no pen?"

Both of us laughed.

"I have all these things inside my huge pockets. Don't worry." Just as the new majority leader offered me a seat, one of the parliamentarians said, "Mr Bah, get out of this office. We are having a meeting about something very important. If you can wait outside until we are done, that is fine. Otherwise, you can fix another appointment time. Get out, now."

I was very perplexed. I could not believe this person was talking to me. I had come on appointment with his boss. The majority leader himself is happy to see me, has welcomed me and has even ushered me to a seat. Who is this man to send me out of an office that is not even his? The owner of the office says, "Welcome" and a visitor like me says, "Get out". I understand that in the course of my journalism, I had stepped on many toes, especially of those in power. This particular parliamentarian could be upset with me for another work I had previously done – and thus reproving the interview with his boss for fear of a possible 'grill'.

I ignored him and went ahead to take a seat. He rose, walked up to me and

121

screamed out once again, "Get out!"

"I'm not going anywhere. Your boss is the only one who can send me out."

"You are rude. You are not going to interview anybody here." His face was less than an inch from mine. I felt threatened because he had motioned his hand in a way as if he was going to slap me.

Another parliamentarian called me aside and took me out to the lobby. He apologized for the misconduct of his colleague on behalf of the country's parliament and on behalf of the majority leader. He asked me not to leave and assured me that my interview was really going to take place.

Moments later, someone came to call me that the majority leader was ready for the interview. The same group of parliamentarians was still in the majority leader's office. My assailant did not say anything to me this time around. He sat silently at a corner while he glowered at me.

Dressed in a shiny blue kaftan, the majority leader once again beckoned me to take a seat while he sat across me, behind a fanciful and shiny wooden desk. He did not talk about the incident that had just happened but was apparently sad about it. In fact, he inquired whether I wanted the interview to be private – with no one except for the two of us in the room. I replied in the negative and set up my mini tape recorder.

As the interview began, the majority leader reveled in his background and achievements. His colleagues seemed to be proud of him and were smiling as he went on self-promoting himself. However, when I started touching on delicate topics such as his and his colleagues' apparent betrayal of his immediate predecessor who was now jailed, I saw the change in mood around the room. Even so, my interviewee stuck to his guns and blamed his predecessor for his tribulations.

I pressed on with the interview asking about the hypocrisy in their actions. I questioned the moral ground of his position against his predecessor as he had also been one of the jailed leader's protégés and had lived a high life – taking preferential help from him such as car loan even when he knew it was not 'clean' money. In addition to already driving a huge and very expensive car; marrying a teenager for a second wife despite being old enough to be her grandfather,

all beyond his earnings were enough questions for him to answer. His face changed. He tried to say some words, but could not. All of a sudden, he began to stammer. When he finally regained his composure, he scorned his friend and mentor as a "blundering fool".

I was not done yet. I had long wanted to expose the influence of religious leaders in national politics and politicians' readiness to worship the ground religious leaders walk on. I had done a thorough investigation about this particular majority leader. He had traveled all the way to Guinea Conakry to spend huge sums of money to meet a certain religious leader for guidance on how to run the parliament. I knew that if I asked him directly, he would deny it, so I flattered him as a widely travelled man. He fell for the bait by mentioning the names of the many countries he had visited. However, he did not mention Guinea Conakry. When I asked him whether Guinea Conakry was among the many countries he had visited, he said yes and I then asked him to name at least one town that he had visited in Guinea Conakry.

He looked as though the life was seeping out of him.

He said he could not pinpoint one particular town as he had visited many places in that country.

Then I jogged his memory by mentioning the town of Basra, and asked whether he had been there before.

He smelled a rat, as he shrugged and hesitated. He tried to say something, looked around the room, and replied in the positive. He apparently began to sense that I knew something about his secret visits to Basra.

Across the room, the rest of the parliamentarians did not sense anything yet. It seemed it was only the two of us who knew where the interview was heading – as they were all smiles and nods in apparent pride at how widely traveled their majority leader was.

I pressed on. When he evaded my question about the purpose of his visit to Basra, I gave him the name of a certain influential religious leader whom he had been visiting in Basra with the explicit goal of helping him through fetish means to be a powerful politician in The Gambia.

The majority leader admitted that he had visited the spiritual leader in question.

There was total silence in the room. His colleagues nodded in silence.

Finally, the majority leader admitted to having consulted that particular religious leader to seek spiritual help for the prosperity of The Gambia and not to cast evil spell on his political rivals.

His response reminded me of the protagonist in the Senegalese writer Aminata Sow Fall's *The Beggars' Strike*, who sought political eminence by pandering to the dictates of a seer.

At the end of 2003, I received the prize of the Most Dynamic Reporter from the Daily Observer.

I returned to Ghana on Tuesday, 22 August 2006. Life continued as usual in Ghana. My daily routine was still the same – going to the MFWA offices to help in their work and keenly follow events in The Gambia on the Internet, and occasionally talking to my family.

I felt increasingly lonely and desperate again. The respite I had by visiting Sweden seemed over. I began battling with the reality of my life yet again. Initial hopes about my possibility to get help from some of the conference participants had shattered as communications between me and them were poor. At some point, I got discouraged at the possibility of getting help and stopped trying to keep in touch. In the meantime, Amie Joof was regularly in touch with me.

She had advised that I enroll in some school in Ghana so that I would be occupied and worry less. She asked me to talk to the head of Media Foundation about it while she would also scout around for possible scholarships. She was very encouraging as according to her, Ghana was a bastion for education in West Africa and that I would be happy, at the end of the day, to utilize my time going to school. I agreed. I began to look around for a school. Occasionally, Mohammed, a staff of the Media Foundation and a good friend, went around town making inquiries about schools.

17

A happy moment beckoned. On Sunday, 17 September 2006 two of my friends from Senegal, Agnes and Sillah, visited Ghana to attend a conference. They are very nice people who took great care of me when I was in Senegal. The last time I saw them was at the airport when I was coming to Ghana. That moment of solidarity made me miss them so much and so eager to see them again. They were staying at Paloma Hotel, not far from where I was living. On the evening of their arrival, I visited them at their hotel. They were waiting for me at the hotel courtyard. The plan was that as soon as we saw each other, we would swiftly leave the hotel, and go to my house. The reason was that there were too many Gambians inside the hotel also attending the same conference. There was no indication that I could trust anyone outside the core people who had been helping me since my escape. Therefore, Sillah and Agnes decided that the hotel was a no-go area for me for just a few days until those particular people left the hotel. In fact, I was terrified to learn about the presence of many Gambians around. I was fearful of the fact that someone could possibly be an agent for the government and meeting them would not be a wise idea because my presence in Ghana was under strict secrecy intended to keep me comfortable and safe from the dictatorship.

It was a sombre moment when I saw them. I ran to them and embraced both of them simultaneously. We kept expressing how happy we were to see each other again, while recalling our last moments at the airport in Senegal.

We went to my room, and stayed there for a long time chatting, and recalling the sad events of my stay in Senegal, while also discussing the terrible state of things back home in The Gambia. When we entered my room, Agnes looked uncomfortable in the room, but she stated that she was happy that I found refuge somewhere farther from home and had wonderful neighbors to help me. She told me to be patient and understand that the Media Foundation was a great and reputable organization that would indeed help me settle down.

The following day, they invited me to a restaurant in town to eat a Ghanaian dish, fufu. They both said that they had been craving fufu. I felt very happy and had a great deal of company during those moments. I saw them every day during their stay and they let me go with them everywhere they were going during their stay.

Friday, 22 September 2006 was a presidential election in The Gambia. I was in Sillah's hotel room while we monitored the results. Sillah was also making calls to his contacts to get regular updates as the election results came in. We were keenly interested in the outcome. That was because a loss for the dictator, Yahya Jammeh, would mean that Gambians who were languishing in exile in various places around the world would return home. That would also herald the return of sanity and freedom in our country.

However, our hopes were shattered because the dictator won with about 67 per cent of the vote. The opposition candidates trailed far behind because more than a third of the voters who were expected to vote for the opposition did not cast their votes. Rampant voter apathy in The Gambia was mostly caused by intimidation by government security forces or due to mere lack of interest.

On his first national statement following the elections, an apparently angry President Jammeh, because of the international criticism, said that nothing could remove him from power and that, "The whole world can go to hell".

Well, that meant I would go to hell too as his victory meant I would continue to be in exile – probably for a long time, or for the rest of my life. It was very sad to think about what the future had for me. Sillah was equally sharing my feeling because, since the burning of his house by security forces for his reporting as a journalist, he had been in exile. He was visibly distressed.

In a corner of the room, I sat on a chair, while watching TV. I stole glances at Sillah from the corner of my eye. I could not figure out the expression in his face but I could guess that he was disturbed about what the future held for Gambians.

"I don't know what I am going to do with my life now," I said, as tears flowed down my cheeks.

Ten days after they arrived, on 27 September 2006, Agnes returned to Senegal. Our farewell was sad and it was hard for me to see her leave. They were all like family to me now. I could not imagine bidding her farewell once again without knowing when to see her again. Before she got into the taxi that took her to the airport, she hugged me once again and gave me some money.

Sillah had stayed behind. He would be in Ghana for another week or so. He was attending another conference that was also organized by the Media Foundation at the same venue. This time around, I was a conference participant. Only one person was coming from The Gambia, Momodou Lamin Jaiteh. He was among the first group that had come earlier, but I could not see him then because he was with many other people. He was the Media Foundation correspondent in The Gambia and had been working in the private media.

During this particular conference, Sillah, Momodou and I were the panelists on The Gambia session. We discussed in detail the sorry state of the media and the appalling human rights situation in The Gambia.

Yet another sad moment came when Sillah left for Senegal on Wednesday, October 4, 2006. Like Agnes who left earlier, he also gave me some money. I felt lonely and increasingly distressed. When he was in Ghana, he had kept me company. Days before he returned to Senegal, he would come to the Media Foundation offices to hang around and go out for lunch with me and some of the staff.

Luckily for me, I still had some sort of company – Momodou's flight back to The Gambia would be two days after the departure of Sillah to Senegal. It was an opportunity for me to have some time with him. We went out in the evening to have fufu and later sat at a restaurant near the main highway watching the traffic and drinking Coca Cola. He also expressed happiness that I was okay and safe in Ghana. He told me that the days following my escape and the government declaring me a 'wanted' man, were very stressful as many people thought that I was dead. According to him, they thought the government had already killed me and were just announcing that I was a 'wanted' person as ploy to make the public believe that I was being sought. He said there was sadness and confusion across the country, especially in the media.

Momodou said that after the initial confusion, rumors started going around town that I had escaped, and alive, and in Senegal. He said that after some time, word started going around that I was in Ghana. According to him, there were some reports that I was living in Spain. I told him that I was in Sweden for about a week but never went to Spain and did not know why someone would suggest that I was there. Momodou said that people within the country were very good at spreading rumors and that some were always eager to spread false information all over the place. He said someone had claimed he had helped me to escape. He said the person in question even claimed that I had slept in his house on my way to Senegal.

These were all false. The two of us went on and on about The Gambia, bemoaning the tyranny and how sad the situation was. When I went home that evening, with the thought that Momodou would be leaving in just a matter of two days, I felt even more miserable. I could not bear the thought that all the people I know from my country were now leaving, which made me lonely and miserable. Momodou's return to The Gambia marked the beginning of another episode of loneliness and uncertainty for me. I yearned for the day when I would be back in my country where I would live like the free person I was before. In the meantime, I was grateful that I had the Media Foundation to help me, and that my Ghanaian neighbors were extraordinarily wonderful people. They took me like family and cared much for me.

I continued to communicate occasionally with some people I had not communicated with for a long time. When I escaped from The Gambia, the only picture of me that was available online belonged to the Washington D.C. based magazine, *Port of Harlem*, for which I was correspondent while in The Gambia. Because the *Freedom* newspaper had been using that particular picture when writing stories about me, the editor of the magazine had contacted them asking for explanation about the use. When he communicated with the *Freedom* newspaper editor, he forwarded the emails to me. That time, he did not even know what was going on with me. *Freedom* gave the *Port of Harlem* editor a brief explanation about the situation. Now, I was glad that he had a clear picture of what exactly was going on with me.

In addition, Ibrahima Diallo from Guinea Conakry had been following my case. I responded to one of his emails that he had sent me several months earlier when I had just escaped from The Gambia. He was so elated to hear from me that he sent me some money and said that it was his contribution toward my welfare. I was at once surprised and grateful for his generosity. The two of us had met some time around May 2005 when he visited me at my *Daily Observer* newspaper office in The Gambia. He was on one of his occasional trips to the country when he decided that he wanted to meet me in person because he had been my ardent fan. I felt honored and humbled. We became very good friends since then and kept on the communication line.

My newest friend in Sweden, Anna Sandquist, whom I met at the conference, had been communicating with me occasionally since I returned to Ghana. She sent me some money, which she said was her and her friends' contribution toward my upkeep.

Despite the overwhelming support and encouragement by some of my friends across the world, I still felt depressed and lonely. I had been falling sick a lot. My health grew so bad that it caught the attention of the staff at the Media Foundation. They had their own doctor at a medical centre called Rabito Clinic. The doctor did several tests on me and gave me some medicine. After some respite, I suffered a relapse. The Media Foundation continued taking me to the same doctor. At some point, I was so frequent at the doctor's that I told the staff not to bother taking me there – that I knew the way and did not need to bother them. I withdrew into myself. Apart from my normal routine to and from the Media Foundation office and interaction with neighbours, I lived like a recluse. An American lady who was a master's degree student was interning at the Media Foundation. When she was returning home to America, she gave me a radio set. The set was a good source of company whenever I was indoors for a long time. Sometimes, I would stay indoors for so long that some of my neighbors would knock at the door to check on me. Sometimes one of the twins next door would ask me to accompany her to the shop and keep her company.

Though it would take time, I occasionally called my family back home. I had news from my elder brother that my father had been very sick. Soon after I spoke with my elder brother, I called my father. His voice sounded different and sickly. He told me that he had not been feeling well for some time but that he was recovering gradually. I never mentioned to him or any member of my family including Teddi about my poor health, as I did not want to distress them.

Some days after my initial call, I followed up to see whether my father was getting better. He sounded much better this time around. We spoke for a little longer than my usual brief calls. He told me my friends, Kanta and Moko, had been visiting the family regularly—at a time when most people had ostracized my family. He added that he would like to visit Amie Joof in Dakar to thank her for taking care of me during my flight from The Gambia.

I was glad to hear that and then asked him to take good care of Teddi for me during that period and to make sure that nothing happened to her.

I continued battling with poor health and began to lose weight. I felt like the medicines that I had been receiving from the clinic were not efficacious, because I felt no better after taking them. I used to feel intense heat in my body. Sometimes, I had to put some water in a bucket or kettle to take a quick shower late at night to cool down my body temperature. This used to happen to me even when the weather was cold. In most nights, high fevers would disrupt my sleep. My head and my feet were always hot as though fire were raging inside them. When this happened, I would put my feet against the cement wall of my room, which was usually cool at night. In some cases, I had to soak my feet in a bucket of water for a long time in order to cool the temperature down, before lying down and pressing them against the cement wall for further cooling.

My doctor, Edmund Delle, was concerned about my numerous visits to Rabito Clinic. He had initially tested me for infections such as Hepatitis B, and

129

Typhoid but found nothing in my body. Therefore, on one of my numerous un-announced visits to the clinic, on October 30, 2006, he asked to have a private meeting with me. During our meeting, he asked me several questions about how I was taking my medicine. I told him that I took my medicine as pre-scribed and that I was worried about what could be wrong with me. He sug-gested I take an HIV test, but he left the decision to me. A chill ran through me, from the top of my head to the tip of my toes. In all my worries, I had nev-er thought of HIV. My eyes felt like pepper and were hurting. I cupped my chin in my hands and furrowed my forehead in deep thought. I realized I was trembling. I had always been afraid to do an HIV test. It was something I al-ways avoided because I did not think I could handle the subsequent trauma if the results turned out to be positive.

However, given my worsening ill health, I thought I should go for it. Be-sides, I could possibly get treatment if the test result happened to be positive. I had decided that whatever happened, I was ready to live with it. I informed Dr Delle of my decision. I also told him that I would like a test of Hepatitis B done on the same day. I had once had a test on Hepatitis B before and was negative but given my deteriorating health, I wanted to leave no stone un-turned. The doctor sent me to the lab for the two tests to be done. After finish-ing with the lab, I was asked to sit in the main lobby to wait for the results. The results would be taken to the doctor who would then tell me the outcomes. I waited for hours, but those hours seemed like forever to me. During that waiting, my head throbbed harder and I was thinking that my life would never be the same again if the results came out bad for me. I waited with my heart in my mouth.

The results finally came.

Someone called me to go into the doctor's office. The short pace from the lobby to the doctor's office took me ages to complete. I felt so exhausted and hopelessly weak that I had to hold on to things while walking toward Dr Delle's office. As soon as I opened the door, he smiled at me and said, "It is negative."

I felt faint.

"What? I don't have HIV/Aids? What…, Doctor!" "You do not have it," he said.

I was covering my mouth with one hand in a pleasant surprise. My left hand was still holding the door. Thrilled with disbelief, I slammed the door closed, jumped on Dr Delle, and embraced him. It was the kind of 'thank you' that is beyond words. After I released him, I shook his hand and expressed my grati-tude to him for helping me because he had given me the courage to go through the testing process.

He gave me a chair and asked me to sit down. He engaged me in a chat. He told me that the Hepatitis B results were also negative. This seemed like a wonderful day for me. Since I escaped from my country, I might have smiled or laughed at some point or the other, but I was beside myself with glee on this particular day. I felt as though I had been nominated for the Nobel Prize.

Dr Delle then asked me about anything I thought might help him to figure out a remedy for my condition. I wanted to tell him my story—my escape and the fear, agony, despair, hopelessness, loneliness… but I hesitated. Like other Ghanaians, I appreciated the help and hospitality he was giving me, but my troubles had made me more cagey and suspicious. I told him nonetheless that I was battling with a lot of stress, which I presumed might be the cause of my failing health.

He looked at me with concern and advised me to avoid stress, as it could be inimical to my health. Thereafter he gave me his business card and asked me to keep in touch so that, on some of his family's occasional trips to the Ghanaian mountains, they would invite me to join them. Finally, he advised me to be more involved in social activities, as that could ameliorate my condition.

Afterwards, my health condition improved gradually. I felt stronger physically and emotionally, but I never called Dr Delle for his family trips to the mountains. However, whenever I saw him during my regular appointments at his clinic, I always thanked him for his support and for helping me to regain self-confidence and faith in life again.

18

Sometime in late 2006, the Media Foundation and its partners were going to organize a conference in Senegal to discuss the deteriorating press freedom and human rights violations in my country. My status as a victim of the dictatorship and my role as the secretary general of the Gambia Press Union made me an ideal participant in that conference. Three people – the head of the Media Foundation, one of his employees, and I were to attend from Ghana.

When I learned about the upcoming trip to Senegal, I became fearful all over again. There was no way I would go to Senegal. I lived there under solitary conditions in fear when I first escaped from The Gambia and was moved out of there because it was too dangerous for me due to its proximity to The Gambia. I could not imagine how anyone could think of me going back there. I wondered who might have come up with such an idea, but I decided right away that I was not going to go. However, the head of the Media Foundation invited me to his office and talked to me about the event, emphasizing that my security would be taken care of and that they would not put me in any sort of danger. He told me that my participation in the conference would be very useful and helpful in the efforts to stop freedom of speech violations in my native Gambia. With a great deal of reluctance, I agreed to go. However, I was still very fearful. I just hoped that nothing went wrong during the trip.

Now that going to Senegal was certain, I thought it was a great opportunity for my wife and some of my family members to sneak across the border and come over to Senegal so that we could see each other. I called my wife but she was bedridden. She had been down with malaria for days, and had even moved to her village to stay with her mother. Her voice was hoarse and I could not make out what she was saying. It sounded like she was in great pain, and thus she would not be able to make it. I could clearly hear her sobbing on the other end of the line. I tried to calm her down, but she would not. After the call, I felt depressed – for her sobbing, for her illness, for her inability to make it to Senegal. Even so, I kept faith and hoped that we would live long and safe to see each other someday.

I got my father on the phone. As always, I could feel the mixture of sadness and happiness in his voice. Since he had once suggested that he wanted to go to Senegal to personally thank Amie Joof for taking great care of me during my flight from The Gambia, I felt this was going to be a perfect opportunity for him to do that and to see me. I explained to him how it was important for them to let no one else know about their trip to Senegal. We agreed that both he and my mother would come. If my wife was not sick, the three of them could have travelled together. My father told me that he would keep checking on her but if she did not travel together with him and my mother, it meant she had not recuperated enough for the journey. I later called my elder brother and gave him the contact information of Amie Joof so that he would give it to our parents for their use when traveling to Senegal.

I had communicated with all my friends who helped me while I was in exile in Senegal. They were all excited and looked forward to seeing me. In addition, just a few days before it was time for me to go to Senegal, my Swedish friend, Katia, called me to say that she had learned from Amie Joof that I would be in Senegal. She told me that coincidentally, she was also scheduled to travel to Senegal at the same time to work on a newspaper story on the dangerous canoe travel that West African youth use to migrate to Europe. I was excited at the prospects of seeing Katia.

It was on a late Sunday evening, December 3, 2006 when my plane touched down at the Leopold Sedar Senghor International Airport on the outskirts of Dakar. Kwame Karikari and his employee Saidou Arji were with me. The three of us followed each other to pick up our luggage from a lobby. We were all conscious of the dangers to my life, so I stayed sandwiched between the two of them just to be sure that I was safer.

As soon as we reached the exit of the airport terminal, I saw my father. His distinguishing features made him stand out. He is slim and tall with a wide forehead, and dark complexioned. He usually wears a kaftan with the round Fula turban that is rolled around the head. He has a defect in one of his eyes and thus always wears dark glasses. In most cases, he always has a shepherd's stick or a simple handbag or both. On this occasion, he had only a handbag. I ran towards him and gave him a bear hug. Seeing any member of my family was one thing I never thought would ever happen in my life again. I released him to look at him just to make sure that I was not dreaming. My father was in the company of a young man about my age, who is Amie Joof's nephew. The airport was crowded, and people were watching the two of us. It was not possible to know whether an abductor was among the onlookers. However, my father's presence reassured me that all was well.

My father was quiet all the time. The two of us shook hands. "How are you, Father?"

No response.

Instead, I saw streams of tears flowing down his cheeks. It was rare to see my father sob. As a result, I grew so tense that I did not know what to say or do. Amie Joof's nephew had already informed him how my trip was going to be – to attend the conference in a hotel outside the capital from Sunday to Wednesday. That was why they had come to the airport so that the two of us would see each other, and my father would return to Amie Joof's house where I would find him when I returned to the city on Wednesday. The two people I came with from Ghana were visibly happy to see my reunion with my father. I could see a sense of pride and happiness in Karikari's face when he shook hands with my father.

"I never thought I would see you in my life again…Omar," my father managed to say in a shaken voice. Tears were still rolling down his cheeks.

"It's okay Baaba." (His name is Samba but I call him Baaba meaning father in my Fula language.)

"I am safe and okay in Ghana. The people you are seeing here are taking very good care of me there. And the people in that country are very good and caring."

He looked miserably helpless about having to live with the fact that his son was being looked after by strangers in a faraway country. He told me that my mother would come with my paternal grandmother as soon as he returned home. We bade farewell and shook hands as we parted.

My colleagues and I got into a waiting minibus with some of the conference participants, while my father and the young man joined a taxi to return to Amie Joof's house.

At the hotel, in a coastal town known as Toubab Dialaw, Amie Joof and Agnes were at the gate to usher us in. "Omar!" I heard someone call. It was Amie Joof. She and Agnes ran toward me. I dropped my bag and rushed to them too. We embraced each other. I was excited to see them again. I had seen Agnes when she and Sillah visited Ghana some months earlier, but this was my first time seeing Amie Joof since I left Senegal. She was grinning widely. She kept expressing how proud she was that I made it to Senegal. They both informed me that safety mechanisms were in place to ensure that nothing happened to me. Besides, many other exiled Gambian journalists were also in the hotel for the same conference. I was glad to get that assurance. I was eager to get to my hotel room so that I could drop my bag and come back to talk to my friends and see my other colleagues. I saw all the exiled journalists who used to keep me company while I was in Senegal. Some journalists and human rights advocates had also traveled from The Gambia to attend the conference. The only exiled journalist I had not seen yet was Sulayman Makalo, who had escaped from The Gambia about a month and a half after my escape. By the time he arrived in Senegal, I had already left for Ghana. I had nonetheless had some email conversations with him, and we were looking forward to seeing each other. It was a beautiful night by the sea in Senegal. Most of the conference delegates were hanging out near the restaurant enjoying the cool breeze. Sulayman joined us. His face lit up when he saw me. We embraced and shook hands. We kept shaking our hands while saying nothing. Everyone was looking at us. At some point, Sulayman said to me, "You are a very lucky person," in reference to how the dictator in my country would have murdered me if he had laid his hands on me. Sulayman was in The Gambia at the time and used to send alerts to the international community about my case. The two of us had been close friends since my early days as a journalist when we used to work together at *The Independent* newspaper. We also attended the same media-training center. He told me how he was emotionally distressed and fearful for my life during the whole drama. The two of us had a lot of catching up to do. I felt even safer now that I had seen someone who escaped after me and was still living inside Senegal. We took a stroll near the waves and kept talking about our respective stories for a long time. Afterwards, we went to the room of one of the conference participants where a group had gathered to brew green tea locally known as attaya or warrga. I enjoyed the company but refused to drink the green tea because I had not had it since I left my country and would not like to return to such an addictive drink – especially when it would be hard to get it in Ghana. The two of us remained inseparable throughout the conference. We hardly slept. We stayed up in our rooms watching TV and talking about our country, and occasionally going to the open courtyard of the hotel.

When the conference opened the following morning, I was happy to have the chance to give my input on the way forward for press freedom in my country. I spoke about the terrible rights violations in The Gambia based on my escape story and on my perspective as secretary general of the main journalists' union. The outcomes of the conference were resolutions, plans and funding pledges to strengthen and make the Gambia Press Union a stronger and more viable organization that would be in a position to stand for persecuted journalists in a more effective way.

At the end of the conference, on Wednesday, 6 December 2006, I went back to the city of Dakar with Amie Joof to her home, where I joined my father who had been waiting for me there for the past days. The moment was nostalgic— both for seeing my father and for stepping inside Amie Joof's home again. My return to her house reminded me of the scariest moments of my life.

My father was very happy to see me. After briefly sitting with Amie Joof and the rest of her family for an exchange of greetings in her living room, my father and I went to his guest room. We needed all the time in the world for ourselves. The expression in my father's face was enigmatic. He looked at the same time worried and relieved – yet he seemed not convinced that he was indeed seeing me. I was equally overwhelmed with all these things myself – and could not state what exactly I was thinking as so many thoughts were swirling around my mind at the same time like a spinning pan of water.

My father sat on the edge of the bed, while I sat on a seat opposite him. As we talked, we both kept looking at each other as if we were never going to see each other in life again – of course, we did not know whether we would ever see each other again. The thought of that alone made me feel weak and hopeless. We both certainly had so many questions for each other. First, he confirmed which country I was actually staying, what direction – east, west, south or north. He also asked about the kind of language they spoke, and the kind of food they ate. As I answered all these questions, my father's face looked like he was worried and about to cry, but I allayed his fears by assuring him that I was safe and well taken care of by both the organization that took me there, and my neighbours in Ghana.

More questions kept coming. He asked me about the whole story – what exactly happened, how I escaped, how I knew Amie Joof and how I ended up in Ghana, et cetera. It took hours before I could explain in detail all the answers to his questions. He was paying close attention. As I talked, tears ran down his cheeks.

"I cannot believe that I am sitting with you right now," he said. "I never thought I would ever see you in my life again."

"Me too, Baaba. I still think I am dreaming, and I still cannot believe that I am seeing you."

"It felt like a dream too, when I saw you at the airport. You have been through a lot, but I am praying for you so that you find safety, my son."

"Thank you, Baaba. I will be fine. Just avoid worrying yourself too much. I have good people taking care of me."

I tried my utmost not to let my father know about my misery because I feared that if he did he would no longer be at ease when he returned home.

I also had infinite questions. My father told me about his arrest and detention for a day shortly after my escape. He said at that time, he did not even know what exactly was going on. He was not also sure whether I was still alive or dead. According to him, he was with some of his friends at a store in Barra grieving over what had happened to me when some security men in both uniform and in plain clothes, armed to the teeth, suddenly came to arrest him. That all the security officials wanted to know was for him to tell them where I was hiding at that moment. He said he told them that he neither knew what was actually happening to me nor knew where I was. According to him, they threatened never to release him if he did not provide them with the information they were seeking. He added that at some point his interrogators told him that they had gotten information that I was currently hiding under the protection of a woman.

"What? They told you that they knew a woman was hiding me. Baaba, that means that these people had information about me, which meant that I was in real danger."

"I thought they were just trying to check whether I would talk - even though I did not know anything about your escape. But now that I know the whole story, I realize that this government had a lot of information about you because the thing about the woman was true since you were hiding here, with Amie Joof."

He warned me to be extra careful in anything I was doing since I must understand that the dictator was seeking my head. According to my father, truckloads of armed security personnel also visited my wife on several occasions. He said they threatened her and kept asking her about my whereabouts too. He told me they continued monitoring her by stalking her with unnumbered security cars and anonymous callers threatening her over the phone. Even though she changed her cell phone number; they still got it somehow and kept harassing and threatening her. The other direct victim of my troubles with the dictatorship was my elder brother, Ebou. My father informed me that Ebou was arrested at the ferry terminal in Banjul because he looked like me. It took a lot of effort and the showing of a series of identification documents before he was released from police detention on the same day.

"We have suffered a lot under this government, Omar. They are still monitoring our movements, threatening us, and causing us a lot of fear and discomfort in the country. In fact, when you initially escaped, we all thought that you were dead. Despite all the suffering you are going through right now, we are happy and relieved that you are alive," he said.

Our chat kept us awake until morning. I was very curious about how everyone was doing. My father updated me with everything. I had missed my wife, all my relatives and fellow villagers. My father told me how people had been good to the family; that the family had received a lot of moral support and solidarity from relatives and villagers. One of the saddest updates my father gave me from back home was the number of deaths that had occurred during just the short period I had been away. Our village chief was among the many people who had died. In addition, the best friend of one of my half-brothers had died from snakebite. He told me so many sad stories about my village and the country at large, that I could not control my emotions. Tears rolled down my cheeks so much that I had to wipe my neck, as it was soaked with tears. By the time my father and I finished chatting, it was daybreak. Our nightlong conversation had been one of the most beautiful moments in my entire life. We were both relieved at seeing each other while at the same time having enough time to talk in detail.

That Thursday morning, on December 7, 2006 was going to be an even sadder day as my father was going to return to The Gambia so that my mother and grandmother would also try to sneak out of the country and come to see me in Senegal. After taking breakfast and exchanging pleasantries with Amie Joof, he took a stroll down to the junction near the main road, a few hundred feet from Amie Joof's house. He had already developed acquaintance with a trader in a small shop there who was from the same Fula ethnic group as we are, and thus, had been hanging out there while I had been at the conference. He was going to bid farewell to that shop owner so that he would return and pack his bag and go. It all felt like it was not true – that the time I had to spend with my father had elapsed; that he was leaving, probably for good without us ever seeing each other in life again. I could not just stand the thought of seeing someone going back to my country – the only place I knew until recently – yet I could not go there. The thoughts were so many in my mind that I did not know what I was thinking. I was sad, and my body was almost motionless. When my father returned from the store and it was time for him to leave, I could see that he was sad but just trying to put a brave face on it. Nevertheless, it had to happen – he must go.

While we stood on the corridor, my father gave me four cassettes of various Fula singers. He knew that my favourite music – that could help keep me company was Fula music especially the one with the violin and/or hoddu (Fula guitar) instruments which many had noticed I was obsessed with. I got that from my father because I grew up in our compound while he was a keen fan of such music. When I escaped from The Gambia some months earlier, I had three of such cassettes in my handbag and they had been helpful in relieving my agony. Because I had over used them, I was now ready for new music that

I had not heard before.

When I gave him part of my per diem toward his transport fare back home, he rejected it outright, saying that he would not mind spending his last penny just to see me repeatedly. Because he had spent so much money on his fare and would be spending even more on my mother and grandmother, I insisted he take the money to defray his expenses. I also gave him a photo I had taken at the conference, which he took from me with reverence, as though it were some relic of his religious faith. He stared at it and then looked at my face – and kept doing so repeatedly for some time and smiled. I tried to force a smile too, but stopped short of showing my teeth. My lips were just so heavy to lift or move. However, I managed to give him the happy look – or so I thought I did.

Before leaving, he thanked Amie Joof profusely for her tender loving care toward me and lavished effusive praise on her generosity and deep humanity. The young man, who had escorted my father to the airport to see me when I arrived in Senegal a few days earlier, was to accompany my father and me to the car park about a mile or so from Amie Joof's house. Though both my father and I were scared that I would be going out, the young man's presence made me feel safe.

As we walked down the sandy roads past the sports stadium, my father and the young man insisted that I should walk between them for my own safety. My father was repeatedly advising me as we walked to be careful wherever I was and have faith in God. Before he boarded a car, he thanked the young man for his unflinching support and help, and asked him to continue to do so. We shook our left hands. The two of us shook hands and continued to hold each other's hand while staring at each other for what seemed to be forever. Then he hopped into the car.

Shortly after that, my mother, grandmother and my younger brother Alhagie whom we fondly called Alhagie Dembo visited me in Dakar. Their visit like that of my father made me at once happy and sad, especially when my grandmother kept saying that she needed to see me because she was getting old and might not see me again before she died. Consequently, I asked her to tell me a didactic story on the eve of their departure to The Gambia.

"It's stories, stories…," she said.

"Yes, indeed," my mother and I responded.

"Once upon a time, there lived a woman who got pregnant out of wedlock which was an abomination in her village. She was ostracized as a punishment and went to live in the forest, where she scavenged for food during the day and slept in a cave inside the trunk of a gigantic tree at night. Because there was no one to help her when she was due to deliver, she did it all by herself. She named the baby boy Essa. Life became tougher for her now that she had a child to feed. She therefore risked leaving the child on his own in the cave during the day, while she went looking for food. The baby would cry all day while the mother was gone.

"On the other side of the same gigantic tree, there was another cave, where a lioness lived. The lioness had a son who was about the same age as the human baby. The lioness' baby was named Samba. The lion cub also used to be by himself all day while his mother went to hunt for food. Essa's constant cries attracted young Samba's attention. Luckily, for animals, they could walk soon after birth. So Samba decided, one day, to inspect the other side of the tree trunk to see what exactly was going on there. He found Essa and the two began to play together and eventually became best friends.

"However, Samba warned Essa to tell his mother never to let the lioness know about their presence in the forest as she would eat both of them up. He nevertheless assured Essa of his unalloyed loyalty and promised to protect him at any cost. He shared his food and toys with Essa when their mothers were away. One fateful day, Essa's mother did not return home. Essa was confused and lonely. The following morning when Samba came over to play with him, he realized that his friend was sad. Samba thought he could make him happy as he had brought a new toy that they could play with. When Samba pulled out the new toy, it was a human breast – Essa recognized it as his mother's breast and wept uncontrollably. He was certain that the lioness had caught up with his mother and eaten her up. As Essa wept, Samba sang:

> Essa, why are you crying?
> Essa, boy, why are you crying?
> My mother brought me a toy
> I brought the toy to share with you
> Now you are crying.
> Essa, why are you crying?
> Essa boy what are you crying?

As soon as Samba stopped singing, Essa stopped crying too. In response to Samba's questions in the song, Essa told his lion friend about what had happened. Samba embraced Essa in consolation and begged him to wipe his tears, as he would recompense the loss of his mother. That night, when Samba's mother returned home, he poisoned her food and she died after eating it. From then onward, Samba moved into Essa's cave and the two lived together like brothers supporting each other and keeping each other company in the vast jungle. Life was normal for both of them until one day when Essa suddenly started crying again. The lion was confused, as he had always tried to make Essa happy. He asked his friend what might be wrong.

> Essa, why are you crying?
> Essa, boy, why are you crying?
> My mother killed your mother.
> I killed my mother for your sake
> Essa, boy, why are you crying?

"Essa told his friend that he had seen a procession of young men from his mother's village nearby, heading to the bush as though they were going for circumcision rites. He told his friend that he was now a big boy enough to undergo the same rite of passage, which was followed by pomp and ceremony. Essa was sad as he did not know how to get the dresses for the ceremony if he were to join the circumcision. When Samba learned of Essa's concern, he asked him to join his age group for the circumcision and assured him that he would provide the dresses for him during the ceremony that would follow. As the big day drew near, Samba wandered to the outskirts of the village where many clothes had been hung out to dry, scared away the women who were doing the laundry and selected the very best dress fit for Essa and returned to the cave. On the day of the welcome ceremony, Essa was ecstatic as he stood out among the lot because of his sartorial elegance. After the ceremonies, he returned to the jungle with Samba and they both continued living together in the jungle. Life was normal until one day when Essa re-enacted his sobbing fit. Again, Samba sang:

> Essa, why are you crying?
> Essa, boy, why are you crying?
> My mother killed your mother
> I killed my mother for your sake
> You wanted to go to circumcision
> I helped you to go to circumcision
> Essa, why are you crying?
> Essa, boy, why are you crying?

"In response, Essa told Samba of his desire to get married as most of his contemporaries had done. As always, Samba took him along a path until they came across the fattest bull in the village, which he pounced on and refused to let go. The villagers tried everything they could to shoo the beast away, but he would not budge. When asked what the beast needed, Essa asked them to present all the young women of marital age for him to make his choice. The villagers immediately gathered all the village girls in front of Essa who chose the girl he was most attracted to, and marriage rites between the two of them were immediately performed. Then Samba released the bull, and together he, Essa and his new wife returned to the jungle. When they arrived, Samba immediately requested to speak with the couple. He thanked Essa for being a great friend and for trusting him. He however suggested to Essa and the new wife to move back to the village, as his wife might never get accustomed to living in the wild with a beast. Essa was sad to part ways with his loyal friend and cried bitterly. He promised never to forget the lion in his life, and to be always grateful for his wonderful friendship. Before Essa and his wife returned to the village, Samba asked him to do two things. One, to place a jar always filled with water at the backyard of his house; and two, never to mention that Samba's mouth stinks.

"Essa agreed and promised to do that for the rest of his life so as to please his best friend. Afterwards, Essa and his wife built a new home and lived happily among the villagers. He felt sad that he could not see his best friend anymore but he had to move on with life. He did exactly as the lion had requested, and thus, always filled the jar in his backyard with water. After so many years, on one fateful night, while Essa and his wife were chatting in the courtyard of their compound he said, 'I wonder where the lion with the stinking mouth is.'

"When he was saying that, the lion was at that time drinking from the jar at the backyard of Essa's compound. The lion was extremely disappointed and embarrassed, and suddenly fell down and died. When Essa went to his backyard and discovered the lion dead, he also collapsed and died. That caught the attention of everyone in the village. When the villagers gathered, they were curious as to what might have happened. They consulted an oracle who gave them an antidote to death. When they performed the antidote as prescribed, both Samba and Essa rose from the death. Samba looked at Essa and said, 'Thank you for such a reward to a best friend. You will never see me again.'

"The lion vanished into the jungle.

"Then Essa turned to the curious villagers and confessed his betrayal of his best friend."

The moral of the story is self-explanatory. I felt my grandmother was obliquely telling me to be forever loyal to the people who are standing by me in my trying moments.

Meanwhile, Katia had been in town with a cameraperson from her newspaper working on her story. I had seen them earlier on and shared a session or two where they interviewed people for their story. On Monday, a day before my mother and the rest were due to return to The Gambia, Katia visited Amie Joof's house to see my mother. Both were very happy to see each other – my mother thanked her effusively (I interpreted for them) for standing by me throughout my ordeal. She particularly thanked Katia for finding someone who understood our language to call her and inform her that I was alive and safe shortly after my escape from The Gambia. Before she left, she gave my mother some money toward her transport back home. My friends – the other Gambian exiled journalists in Dakar – as usual, made regular visits to spend time with my mother, grandmother and me.

On the morning of Tuesday, 12 December 2006, my mother and grandmother set out to return home to The Gambia. (My younger brother had left earlier). The two had been in Senegal with me for three days now

19

My stay in Senegal, a total of eleven days, was now over. Amie Joof's nephew and I went to an airline office to confirm my flight a day before my departure. My main reason for going there was just to be sure that the airline, which had its main offices in The Gambia, would not have a stopover in Banjul. I understood that the airline usually had brief stops in The Gambia even if it was not in its schedule.

One woman, a staff of the airline, recognized my Gambian Wollof accent and said, "What is the problem with going through The Gambia? It's your country."

I was scared and demanded a refund so that I could get another flight from another airline.

Apparently taken aback by my reaction, she asked for forgiveness and said she was merely joking. By now, the manager had intervened. Even then, I insisted on getting my money back. It was not until they both reassured me that the plane would not stopover in Banjul that I left the office for a nearby store to buy gifts for my neighbours back in Ghana. I bought some pieces of clothes for some of the neighbours, and cow legs – most of them had specifically asked me to bring them cow legs for use in their fufu dishes. Near Amie Joof's house, there was a grill shop where a specially grilled kind of meat lo- cally known as 'dibi' was prepared. I bought that for the people at the Media Foundation office. Now, I was all set, as I had gotten all the things I needed for gifts back in Ghana. Thus, on Thursday, 14 December 2006, the young man took me to the airport to catch an early-morning flight back to Ghana.

Before I left for Senegal, there had been some hint of my being resettled in America. A journalist from the Ivory Coast, Daniel, had been resettled there shortly before I went to Senegal. His fellow Ivorian, Siriki, was in line for possible resettlement. Luckily, for me, before he travelled to America, Daniel had helped introduce me to the American refugee resettlement process when he visited the office to say goodbye. When he was leaving the office that day, he asked me to follow up for a brief discussion. He gave me more details about the process and his discussion with the Media Foundation office. I jumped and embraced him like a child given gifts of candies. He told me that given the seriousness of my case, it might take only a couple of months for me to see myself in America for resettlement. I could not believe my ears.

According to him, the Media Foundation officials were not familiar with the refugee resettlement process but assured me that the American Embassy would give them all the information they needed to help me in the process. Daniel had given them the contact information of one Monica Robertson, a liaison officer at the refugee affairs section at the U.S. Embassy in Accra.

I repeatedly thanked Daniel and prayed that he and his family had a wonderful journey to America. After talking with Daniel, a top official of the Media Foundation called me into her office for a discussion. She repeated all the things that Daniel had told her. She expressed hope that I could be lucky to be resettled in the United States – since Daniel was already about to travel, and Siriki was also in the middle of the process. However, she asked me to go home and ponder over the issue for three days before giving her a response on whether I was interested or not. I wanted to say right then and there that I was interested. However, I respected her request and waited for three days. As soon as I gave her my answer following the three-day moratorium, she contacted Monika at the American Embassy to introduce my case as advised by Daniel. Therefore, when I travelled to Senegal for eleven days early in December 2006, the Me- dia Foundation called me there asking for my personal information such as date of birth.

Upon my return to Ghana, I was invited to the Overseas Processing Entity (OPE) where I sat down with a caseworker who interviewed me about my personal information, family history, and about my case. The caseworker would use that information to arrange and present it in a coherent way that would be acceptable and easily understood by the immigration officials who would be coming from Washington D.C., to interview me. I spent probably hours with my caseworker talking about what had happened to me. She made it clear that her position was just like an advocate for me so that my case would be properly prepared.

I did not know when I would be invited for an interview with the American immigration officials who were to come from Washington, D.C. but I was excited at the prospects of meeting them. The mere glimpse of a better future for my battered life was a tonic to me.

Suddenly, things started to look up. On January 3, 2007 the *Freedom* newspaper website named me 'Man of the Year 2006'. In announcing my award, the *Freedom* Newspaper ran the following announcement:

FREEDOM NEWSPAPER'S MAN OF THE YEAR 2006–OMAR BAH

If the Gambia's current picture was to be seen through the decent goggles of International journalism, Omar Bah deserves a gold medal for himself and this noble job. Omar has been a sharp razor ready to skin public officials, particularly those who think they should always inhale the air of special treatment. Omar Bah never spared these sacred cows. He skinned them with 'biting' questions. Omar although young was/is a thorn in the foot for President Jammeh, his CHIAKAS and the NIA. He was certainly the next target in line after Deyda was slayed two years ago. Despite endless death threats Omar stayed the noble course without fear or favor.

As soon as the hacking of the *Freedom* newspaper became an international issue, Omar's candidature of enemy number one for Yahya Jammeh's CHIAKAS and NIA was once again renewed, therefore qualifying him to be chopped within Jammeh's abattoir if he was to be captured! This became more certain. The poor journalist was already on Jammeh's list of "bad eggs". He was being surveyed and followed by the CHIAKAS well before the story of the hacking of the US Based paper became alive. As soon as Jammeh and his gang of killers were aware of the fact that Omar's name was found within those who communicated with the paper's editor it automatically justified a clear cut route for their killing machine to follow him.

What crime Omar committed is not the issue.... The issue is based on a cooked version targeting a seasoned and brave journalist. He was framed by a regime that framed and killed his mentor Deyda Hydara. This very regime hated Deyda's guts equally as they hate Omar's. If they could kill Deyda for opening the Point anniversary party, where he met and talked to Western diplomats then Omar was also going to be butchered for communicating with a critical paper like this one. Any slightest chance for the vampires with bayonets and bullets was enough for them to slay Omar without any remorse. For Yahya Jammeh's regime journalists like Omar Barrow, Deyda Hydara and Omar Bah deserve being buried alive. Was it or is it a crime for anyone to communicate with Pa Nderry M'bai the editor of the *Freedom* newspaper? Where decency and the rule of law exist, it is not a crime. However, where whims and caprices of a blood hungry regime are ruling, it is indeed a crime. Under Yahya Jammeh's rule crime means exposing his callous nature. This same thread led to the death of late Deyda Hydara. This same thread sent many other Gambian journalists into exile, lest we forget the reason why Pa Nderry, Ndongo Sillah and others are far away from home. Under President Jammeh, journalism means subversion. Omar's escape was meant to be because God saved him like he saved his colleagues. His name was being announced for days on the state controlled media outlets. Was that right? The same microphones wanted to criminalize decent souls like Halifa Sallah in 2006. These very cheap journalists at the GRTS and *Daily Observer* are aiding and abetting Yahya Jammeh to justify the operations of his killing machine.

Omar Bah escaped from these killers, took refuge in Dakar and then eventually found his way to another side of the world where tolerance is part of existence unlike The Gambia under Yahya Jammeh where intolerance means bravery.

In view of the above, this paper is so pleased to declare Omar Bah former reporter in The Gambia MAN OF THE YEAR 2006.The management and staff of this paper are therefore extending their best wishes and special prayers to Omar Bah, his immediate family and all those who suffered from the hands of the Jammeh regime following the hacking of this paper in 2006.

To those who suffered because of this criminal act from a desperate regime we say to you THANK YOU FOR BEING THE SHIELDS THAT STOOD TO DEFEND A NOBLE COURSE. TYRANNY SHALL FALL! YAHYA JAMMEH SHALL CRAWL AND WEEP AFTER HIS GREAT FALL! CRY FREEDOM GAMBIA!

Freedom Managing Editor Pa Nderry M'bai describes Mr Bah's award as a victory for Gambian journalists and pro-democracy activists across the globe." Mr. Bah put his life on the line to expose a despotic and totalitarian government in The Gambia, even though the environment for local journalists in that country is not

147

conducive. Bah contributed immensely not only in improving the paper's editorial content, but also to market its image in The Gambia and beyond. He is one of those patriotic sons and daughters of our beloved country, who are ready to die for The Gambia for the sake of press freedom and democracy. Bah survived a state sponsored manhunt to possibly take his life if arrested. He was being hunted by the Gambian state because of his association with the *Freedom* Newspaper. Thank God, enemies of freedom could not lay their hands on Bah. We at the *Freedom* Newspaper are proud of Omar Bah and therefore thought it necessary to register our sign of appreciation to his valuable services to this leading paper by naming him the "Paper's journalist of the Year. Please join me to thank Mr. Bah for receiving such a prestigious award.

According to Mr M'bai, Mr Bah was one of those Gambian journalists to be relied upon "as he served *Freedom* honestly, faithfully and with high degree of responsibility. He was very committed to his work. As our Banjul Bureau Chief, cum Editor, Bah was also charged with the responsibility of overseeing local stringers and other editorial functions. Stories okayed must pass through him before we went to press. We are concerned about *Freedom*'s reputation and as such we always ensured that stories are well researched before publication. Many organizations use *Freedom* for research including US-based universities. Thanks to Mr Bah, *Freedom* is today rated as one of the best online papers on the worldwide web. The management of the paper appreciates his dedication to duty. He is an asset to the *Freedom* Newspaper. We would be doing a disservice to our profession if we fail to acknowledge his outstanding performance in elevating this paper to higher heights."

Finally, Editor M'bai also thanked the paper's staff for their valuable services. "The paper's subscribers suffered all kinds of persecution from the Jammeh government. Some were tortured and forced to leave the country because of their association with the *Freedom* Newspaper. We have no doubt in our mind that Omar Bah and other editorial staffers of this paper were going to be killed if the Gambian state succeeded in laying their hands on them. We are resolute and shall not give into intimidation. We urge Omar Bah to keep up the good work," said Editor M'bai.

Signed,Chief Editor *Freedom* Newspaper
Pa Nderry M'bai

Yet another piece of good news came my way. My friend and colleague, Sulayman Makalo, whom I had just seen in Senegal during my recent travel, was thinking of joining me in Ghana. He had informed me that he was contemplating going to South Africa through the help of some organizations that were sponsoring him. After seeing me in Senegal, and after my continuous pressure, he started to have two minds between South Africa and Ghana – and he finally settled for Ghana. I was happy about his final decision. He contacted the leaders at the Media Foundation about his decision who in turn asked me whether I could share my room with him. Immediately after I confirmed to them, I informed Sulayman so that he could finalize his flight arrangements.

Mid-afternoon of 8 February 2007, a staff at the Media Foundation, Richard (who had picked me up at the airport when I first arrived) and I picked Sulayman up from the Ghana main airport. It was quite a somber moment – to welcome someone whom I knew had similar experiences as I, and someone with whom I could share my troubles. We shook hands and smiled. The three of us took a taxi and headed to my room in town. While in the taxi, I explained to him the kind of room I had and hoped he would find the place comfortable given the size. He said he did not mind and that he would be comfortable living anywhere.

When we arrived, Richard returned to the Media Foundation office, while the two of us stayed at home to rest and for me to introduce him to the neighbors. It was until the following morning that I took him for the first time to the Media Foundation office. From then on, Sulayman did just like I was doing – getting up in the morning to go to the Media Foundation office and interact with neighbors. Occasionally, we would buy calling cards and briefly talk to our respective families back home.

One night, while Sulayman and I were sitting at the tailoring shop of Kakra, I felt like I wanted to take a walk. It was getting late, but I decided I would go. On most occasions, Sulayman and I would do such walks together. However, on that particular occasion, he did not feel like doing so I went down the hill, toward the Media Foundation office. I did not know where I was going. At some point, I decided to go to a cybercafé to check my emails and to read Gambian news online.

When I checked the time, it was almost midnight. I was scared, as I should not have stayed out that late by myself. Recently, vigilante in my neighborhood caught two young men allegedly committing armed robbery. They were beaten and burned to death. From then onwards, Sulayman and I had been very careful about our movements especially at nights. I rushed out of the cybercafé and up the road, heading back home. I walked so fast that I felt like I was running. When I was up the hill, a group of youths approached me speaking in some local language that I did not understand. I noticed that some of them were wielding machetes. The wandering of a young man at such an odd hour who did not understand what people spoke obviously attracted suspicion as a possible armed robber. They were all speaking at the top of their voices at the same time – some of them using the word, 'foreigner' to address me. Their pejorative term did not offend me because even in my native Gambia, the same derogatory term was often used against fellow Africans from other countries. As the group charged closer, I took to my heels. They ran after me. Faced with a matter of life and death, I ran as fast as wind, scuttled into my room and locked it. When I was entering the compound where I lived, I did not hear any noise behind me – perhaps my pursuers had stopped pursuing me

– but I did not take chances and neither looked back nor stopped running. When I got inside my room and locked up, I stood by the door to peep outside to make sure my pursuers were no longer around. Then I noticed my room was empty. Sulayman had not returned home yet. I called his cell phone and he told me that he was still at Kakra's shop. I must have passed the shop at top speed because I did not even notice it was open. As we spoke over the phone, Sulayman noticed that I was breathing fast and asked whether I was okay. I told him that I could not talk right then because I was scared as some people were chasing me. He told me that they might have gone as he was looking out the street but there were no signs of people in the vicinity. I told him to give me some time to regain my breath. After lying on my bed for some minutes, I decided to slowly open the door and went to the shop to join Sulayman. He and Kakra looked relieved when they saw me. They told me that my chasers did not reach the vicinity of my residence, but warned that I should stop the kind of night walks that I just did. As they spoke, I just nodded and promised them that I would never go out alone especially at that time of the night. I was still exceedingly scared. After some minutes, Sulayman and I went back to our room.

The street leading to the home where I was living was narrow and very dark at night. It seemed some people with ulterior motives had been using the cover of darkness and the isolation of the street to do bad things there repeatedly. We would sometimes wake up and find human feces strewn all over the street, which became a great cause for concern for the neighbours who asked everyone to be vigilant and to protect the neighbourhood. I was particularly very scared and started staying indoors once it got dark. The neighbours suspected the nuisance to be the handiwork of some 'feces disposers'. Some people did not have conventional toilets and used buckets for toilets at home instead. After filling such bucket toilets, they would hire such feces disposers to empty the buckets at night. The feces disposers faced a difficult job as no one wanted such disposals to be deposited in their neighborhoods. In fact, they hid and never allowed anyone to see them while they were on mission. Unbeknown to the disposers though, neighbours in my dark and isolated street had mounted vigilante. As expected, one night, they caught one young man late at night carrying a bucket full of feces. They pounced on him and began beating him mercilessly. Before long, dozens of people were on him. He screamed until he could no longer cry. Huge crowds gathered as the beating continued. The young man lay belly-up in the middle of the street surrounded by his assailants. He looked like he was dead to me, but now and then I saw some part of his body move. I could not stand seeing a person being beaten to death. I asked some of my neighbours whom I recognized among the crowds to beg the assailants to pardon the victim. When I told them, they quietly warned me never to repeat that again, as according to them, the assailants could turn on me if they suspected that I was sympathizing with the feces disposer. As if the beating was not enough, the assailants spread the feces that the victim had in his bucket all over his body. In addition, they lit some fire and wanted to burn him alive. When I saw them preparing the fire, I screamed at the top of my voice. "Please don't do that! Please forgive him!"

As soon as I said that, a group of young people surrounded me, threatening to beat me up. Most of them however recognized me, though they were visibly disappointed in my behavior. My closer neighbours, who had earlier warned me about the possible dangers of intervening in such a matter, pleaded on my behalf and thus rescued me from the mob. They took me to my room and asked me to lock my door and never to get out for the rest of the night. I wept, thinking about the possibility of the young man being killed. I just could not stand the thought of someone being killed in cold blood because I knew a similar or worse experience could have happened to me if the thugs in my own country had captured me. I barely slept that night, as I was both bitter about the mob justice on the young fellow and fearful for my life. My friend, Sulayman and I were alert as we thought our room would be attacked that night. When I asked about the victim the following morning, my neighbours told me the drama I created might have worked for him because the mob did not kill him after all. Instead, the mob made him pick the feces and carry his buck- et out of the neighbourhood. However, my friends admonished me once again to be extra careful and never to get near such events again, let alone try to be a peacemaker.

20

My refugee status case had been progressing smoothly. I had been given an appointment to attend an interview with some immigration officials who had come from Washington, D.C. The interview would be taking place in the same place I had had my prep interview with officials of the OPE. On the day of the interview, the office complex was filled with a huge crowd – mostly Liberian refugees who were also being processed for possible resettlement to America. A woman in the company of an interpreter interviewed me. The interpreter was not required because the immigration official who was interviewing me understood my accent. Nevertheless, he was in the room any way – just in case.

The interviewer asked me everything that my caseworker with the OPE had asked before. I repeated the same information. She looked like a very nice person. I could see in her facial expressions that she felt very sorry for me and was particularly concerned. However, she was emphatic about a particular answer, and her emphasis showed that she was dissatisfied with my response. The question was whether I had ever applied for an American visa. I told her that, apart from my recent travel to Sweden while I was already in Ghana, I had never had cause to apply for a visa anywhere. So the answer was 'no' I had never applied for an American visa before. Then she asked me whether I had ever been inside the American Embassy in The Gambia, and for what reason. I explained to her that I had been at both the embassy and the ambassador's residence in my capacity as a journalist. Then she told me that she had information that I had applied for an American visa in 1998. I was astonished to hear that.

"Me?" I said.

She added that someone with the same names and date of birth applied for an American visa back in 1998. Because I stood my ground, she asked other questions.

At the end of the interview, I walked out of the room hoping that the visa questions she was asking about were just interview tactics and nothing more. When I was running *Bantaba*, I had often employed the same tactics to make my interviewees talk. Therefore, I was not worried. I knew I had given her my honest response. I was a man in trouble and in desperate need of help to get to safety. Thus, I definitely would have confirmed that I was the visa seeker in question if I was indeed the one. When I was in the lobby, just across from the interview room, the woman who had just interviewed me stood by the door. She looked like she was waiting, or that she wanted to say something more to me. However, she was silent. I had my fingers printed, and pictures taken by other immigration officials. It seemed that I was done for the day. I did not need to do anything more except to go home and wait for either an approval or denial.

However, as I was about to walk out of the lobby, my interviewer called me, and I followed her into the same room where she had interviewed me earlier. The interpreter followed us in, but she told him that it was not necessary, as she understood my English. He followed us in anyway. The interviewer told me to try to tell her the truth if I were the one who did that particular visa application in 1998. According to her, if the U.S. government found out that I was indeed the one, my whole resettlement case risked being rejected.

Again, I told her that I was not the one. Then she asked me whether I had never even applied for a student visa, I replied in the negative. She told me that applying for a visa was not a problem, but providing the U.S. government with wrong information was wrong. She was talking with visible concern in her face. I told her that I understood what she was saying and that she was concerned, but I could not say 'yes' to something that was actually 'no'. Seeing that she was deeply concerned, I explained to her that even though it might sound unbelievable to her, it was possible that someone else with the same surname and forename might have applied for that visa in question in 1998 because both names are common in The Gambia and in neighbouring countries. Then she reluctantly excused me to go.

On my way home, while in a taxi, I now had a strong feeling that something might be wrong somewhere. Initially, I had thought that the woman was just using interviewing tactics but I now realized that she meant what she was saying for her to call me for the second time. Though more worried than before, I remained steadfast and confident that I would get a positive decision from the

U.S. government because I knew that all the information I provided was accurate and adequate.

After my interview with the immigration officials from Washington, D.C., I did not hear from the embassy for a while. By now, people in the Media Foundation office were constantly asking me about the progress in my case. They seemed astonished that I had not heard from the U.S. government since my interview with the immigration officials. I was now getting pessimistic about the prospects of being resettled in America. However, Daniel Kouaho, the Ivorian journalist who had asked the Media Foundation office to present my case to the U.S. Embassy in Accra occasionally called me from America where he was now residing with his family. He was worried that my case seemed to be in limbo. He advised me to talk to the heads at the Media Foundation so that they could in turn contact the embassy about the seeming silence on my case.

As a result, one morning, heeding Daniel's advice, I walked into Jeannette's office one of the top officials of the Media Foundation and requested to talk to her. I told her about the visa issue that came up during my interview. She told me that she would call Monica at the American Embassy to see what was happening. Some days later, Jeannette told me that she had spoken to Monica who told her that there was a security investigation on my case, which had to be concluded first. She did not say any further and I did not ask any questions.

I was getting very sick again. Actually, I had never stopped being sick since I escaped from my country. But this was getting very serious like the situation that warranted my test of HIV some months earlier. My stomach, as usual, was running continuously. My head pained a lot and I felt like I had fever all the time. I was visiting Rabito Clinic regularly. I was given different kinds of medication that I took as prescribed. Sometimes, when my medication was finished, I would buy malaria tablets or fever tablets from nearby pharmacies to take.

Sulayman was worried about my health. He advised me sometimes to ignore the medicines since they seemed not to work and just wait until I returned to the doctor.

"Boy, I'm sick. I have to take medicine. I don't know what to do," I would tell him. Sometimes he would ask me to go for a stroll with him just so we did not stay indoors, thinking too much about our troubles.

I occasionally called home to speak with my wife and other relatives. As before, I never let them know about my poor health. I did not tell them about the fact that my resettlement process was stalled either. In fact, they knew little about my resettlement process to the United States. I was longing for the day it would be approved and then tell them about the whole thing.

In April 2007, I received a call from Monica Robertson at the American Embassy in Accra, who told me that my case had been approved and then invited me to her office at the embassy. Rather than having me go to the OPE office to receive my letter of approval as other refugees usually did, she instead sent her driver to go there and pick it up for me. When I went to the embassy, I went through the normal security screening. After just a brief wait, Monica came in and walked me to her office. She was very cordial and seemed like she was very happy that my case was a success now. I was equally happy. I imagined my new life in liberty, as against the life of fear and intimidation I had been through these past months so much so I was not allowed to talk with my wife freely. I grinned at the thought of possibly being reunited with Teddi someday. I sat in the lobby of her office while we waited for her driver to return from the OPE with my approval letter. On the other side of Monica's office, across from the lobby where I was waiting, there was another office with a male occupant. He rose once and walked past the lobby, slightly looked at me and waved with a sound like 'hi'. Given the description that Daniel used to give me of him, I rightly guessed that he was Nate Bluhm, the head of the refugee section. Daniel had spoken highly of him and said that he was an ultra generous and highly professional man. I was glad to get to see him. After some time, the driver entered the lobby with my letter. Monica took it from him and proudly handed it to me.

With the deepest feeling of humility and gratitude, I received the letter from Monica and thanked her once again. She walked me to the exit of the embassy and shook my hand again while I thanked her repeatedly. As I walked down the road to pick up a taxi to return the Media Foundation office, I opened the envelope just to confirm my approval by the U.S. government. There was jubilation at the Media Foundation office when I arrived that day. Everyone was happy and relieved that I was finally sure of going to the land of liberty.

From the day I received my approval letter onward, I was involved in a series of events that were part of the preparations for my travel. I underwent a three- day class of American way of life known as 'Cultural Orientation' at the OPE. I also went through the usual medical check-up. It seemed like things were moving very fast now. Daniel would call me from America constantly to ex- press how happy he was and to ask me to start packing as according to him I could be told my travel date any time. He told me that it was important to pack my things because the travel notice dates are usually within a week or so. He was right. I knew I was going to travel to America exactly about a week before the date.

By now, I was no more dealing with the OPE, but another organization known as the International Organization for Migration (IOM) which was the one to coordinate my travel arrangements. Therefore, I frequented the IOM office especially the week before my departure.

A day before my departure, I was called into the IOM office to sign some travel loan papers, and to be told about the time I should be at the airport lobby. However, I was more concerned about one thing – I did not know where in America I was going. I remember when the U.S. immigration official interviewed me, I was asked about relatives of mine who were living in America and I gave the names of my two uncles whose residential addresses I did not know. Therefore, I was wondering, in the absence of such information, what place they would take me. After waiting for some time in the lobby, someone called me and led me into another part of the office. As we walked along the corridor, I asked him, "What place am I going to in America?"

The man stopped briefly, looked at me and said, "Oh, you are going to Providence."

"What? Where is that?" I said.

I was baffled. I had never heard that name before. It sounded to me as something religious or so. The names I had been hearing were places like New York, Atlanta, California, Washington D.C, Chicago or Boston.

"That is the capital of Rhode Island," the man said.

I was wondering what was wrong with that man. He seemed not to notice the surprise in my face and tone at all. He was talking as if he were talking to someone who was familiar with America.

"Is that an island?"

"No. It is a State." He gave me a look with a half grin as if I were some bushman out of the woods. I still had more questions any way – so I pressed on. "It's a State…. What part of America is that?"

Instead of answering my question, he asked me to follow him. After a few paces, he showed me a huge American map attached against a wall. When he pointed at the spot of the state of Rhode Island, the first thing I noticed was its considerably little size as compared to the rest of the United States. Anyway, I was somehow relieved that I now knew where I was going. What I did not know was who chose that place for me and why. Probably I would know later – or at least be able to guess when I got there.

It was mid-afternoon. My friends at the Media Foundation were constantly calling. They wanted me to come back as soon as I could. I was feeling dizzy due to the malaria treatment medicine that refugees were given before departure, but I was happy, filled with exuberance and hope. That was the first time I felt so hopeful in a long time. When I arrived, everyone was waiting. There was a surprise farewell party for me. The tables were laid and the different varieties of delicious Ghanaian dishes provided a beautiful aroma in the air. As we ate, my friends, mostly the professor, repeatedly advised me about how to be mindful and to be focused – that America was a place of opportunities and I could rebuild my life and even have a better one if I kept my focus.

On the night before my departure, Sulayman and I were exceedingly emotional. We could not stand the fact that we were going to be separated. We had kept each other company in our distress. I had been in Ghana before him and I knew what it was like to be alone. However, there was hope for him too as his case was being processed by the American embassy. I wondered how he would cope in my absence. That night, we did not sleep. We kept talking all night, recalling our terrible experiences and our early days in journalism. I wondered when I would have the chance to practice journalism in life again, especially in my own country. Sulayman and I went on and on about our memorable moments in journalism. We both seemed to be bemoaning the quick end to our journalism careers. However, we kept encouraging each other, hoping that the ideals of journalism would not entirely succumb under the dictatorship in our country.

Personally, I still thought the whole thing about my life in the past year was just a very long dream but the truth was that my career as a journalist in The Gambia was over, at least for now. I looked forward to the future, to my new life in America hoping to regain the freedom I had lost and do whatever work I wanted to without hurdles, as is the case in my own country.

I got to the airport very early. It was on the morning of Thursday, 24 May 2007. There was a group of Liberian refugees and travel guide officials already gathered at the airport lobby. I joined them. Sulayman and Kakra, one of the twin sisters who lived next door, had accompanied me to the airport. Before they left, Sulayman and I did a final farewell. We shook each other's left hand.

"Boy, you will also come," I said.

I watched the two of them walk out of the airport. We waved at each other at intervals until they hopped into a taxi.

As I sat in a window seat of a Delta airliner bound for America taking my last glimpse of the beautiful landscape of Ghana, my home for almost a year, I was filled with nostalgia. Occasionally, when I felt so down and quiet, Karikari would ask me whether I was okay. During such conversations, even though I insisted that I was okay, he could tell that I was sad and depressed.

Then he would tell me: "Omar, don't worry. At the end of the day, you will see that good can come out of evil."

I knew that if there was any accurate definition of 'evil', my predicament in the past year was just it. As the plane cruised over the clouds, the professor's words became more meaningful to me: I was headed for America—free and safe forever. That was the good that came out of it.

Endnotes

[1] Kulenteng trees are huge tropical trees whose lifespan is believed to be hundreds of years or more.

[2] Dooki is a fruit tree that grows in the wild and mostly eaten by monkeys.

[3] Daa means mother in my Fula language.

[4] Na nga def is the Wollof greeting for, 'How are you?'

Index

Index

P
Pa Nderry M'bai, 1, 2, 15, 27, 95, 147, 148
Pa Sallah Jeng, 118, 119
Pap Saine, 19
Port of Harlem, 128
President Yahya Jammeh, 2, 16, 17, 30, 31, 58, 59, 70, 90, 91, 95, 119
Professor Kwame Karikari, vii, 85, 94

R
Rabito Clinic, 129, 154
Radio 1 FM, 22, 92
Ramatoulie Charreh, 24, 25
Reporters Without Borders, 24, 69, 70, 71, 72
River Gambia, 11, 62, 79

S
Sainabou Fofana, 5
Sam Mbollet, 3, 4, 6, 10, 11, 42, 47, 53, 54, 78, 96
Sam Sarr, 18
Sana Sabally, 119
Serrekunda Health Centre, xi
Sheriff Bojang Junior, vii, 32, 33, 35, 49, 66, 112
Siriki Diabate, 108
Speaker Sherif Dibba, 28
Stockholm Arlanda Airport, 116
Stockholm, 115, 116, 117
Strike, 23, 123
Sulayman Makalo, vii, 18, 19, 82, 135, 149
Swaebou Conateh, 18

T
T – Centralen, 116, 118
Teddi Jallow, v, vii, 14
Teddi, 5, 14, 37, 97, 110, 111, 114, 129, 155
The Gambia Armed Forces, xii
The Gambia Media Support (GAMES), 18
The Gambia Radio and Television Service, 18, 88
The Independent, ix, xi, 14, 17, 18, 19, 57, 61, 62, 65, 77, 82, 90, 92, 135
The Leopold Sedar Senghore, 133
The Managing Director of the Daily Observer Dr Saja Taal, 22, 25, 71

Index

Manufactured by Amazon.ca
Bolton, ON